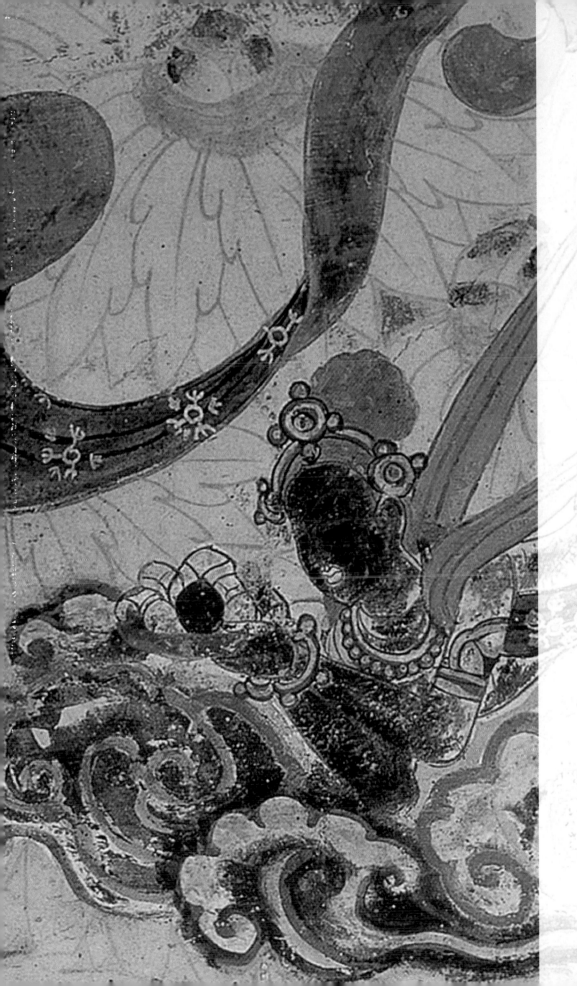

敦煌石窟珍品

Treasures of Dunhuang Grottoes

敦煌石窟珍品

出版：　香港廣彙貿易有限公司

版次：　2002 年修訂本初版發行

　　　　ISBN 962-85787-2-3

Treasures of Dunhuang Grottoes

Publisher:　Polyspring Co., Ltd.

　　　　　　2002 Revised first edition

　　　　　　ISBN 962-85787-2-3

目録● CONTENTS ●目次

窟四十二個，壁畫四千二百多平方米，彩塑二百五十九身，是除莫高窟之外的最大一處石窟群。特別是那高達 24.35 米的善跏佛像，那長達 13 米的臥佛，真是氣勢磅礡，宏偉壯觀。還有那清新疏朗、精美絕妙的第 25 窟中唐時的壁畫和那第 2 窟西夏時期的水月觀音；皆被技藝高超的古代藝術大師們妝扮得神韻怡人，華麗多彩，燦爛輝煌。再者就是那堪稱世外桃園的西千佛洞：西千佛洞，位於今敦煌市城西南 35 公里處的党河北岸斷崖上，是敦煌石窟重要的石窟群之一。遺存各時期洞窟二十二個；即北魏二個，北朝一個，西魏一個，北周四個，隋代三個，初唐三個，中唐一個，晚唐三個，五代二個，回鶻一個，元代一個；壁畫九百一十平方米，彩塑五十三身。這些洞窟的造像和壁畫都十分精美，尤其是那一幅幅傳神動聽的故事畫，聽後絕對讓您流連忘返。此外，還有那安西縣城南五十公里處的榆林河下游水峽口石窟、橋子鄉南三十五公裏處峽谷兩岸上的東千佛洞，玉門鎮九十公里左右的昌馬河（疏勒河區域中的一段）處昌馬石窟，肅北蒙古族自治縣城以西二十公里處浪彎北崖上的五個廟石窟、一個廟石窟。這些石窟內容豐富，壁畫精美絕倫，觀後叫您會更加如醉如癡，也是敦煌石窟不可或缺的一部分；它在中國五千年的文明史中，亦屬璀璨的明星，在世界藝術的百花苑中，更是獨樹一幟。因此，敦煌石窟被譽為是中華民族的藝術瑰寶，人類文化遺产的重要組成部分。

敦煌壁畫是宣傳佛教思想的宗教藝術。主要有尊像畫、神怪畫、本生故事畫、因緣故事畫、说法圖、經變畫、佛教史跡畫、供養人畫像和裝飾圖案等；這都是依據佛教經典繪製而成的，並由古代藝術大師們根據當時現實社會生活來塑造神靈、人物形象和生活場景的，從而反映了曲折、生動地故事情節和內容，是研究中國政治、經濟、軍事、建築、美學、文化及社會風貌等翔實而又豐富的形象資料；因而，它們又直接、間接地反映著不同時代、不同民族、不同階層的社會历史。敦煌壁畫內容之豐富，堪稱"牆壁上的博物館"。在結構、布局、人物造形、線描勾勒、賦彩著色等方面都系統地反映了各個時期的藝術風格，以及中西藝術交融的历史面貌。這些，都是舉世無與倫比的。

　　敦煌彩塑是通過雕塑的藝術形像來宣傳佛教思想的。它主要表現的是宗教神像，並運用以高浮雕、圓浮雕、浮雕（影塑）等多種手段與形式：其題材有佛、菩薩、弟子、天王、力士、僧人、天獸、飛天、伎樂天等。大者有三十四米高的巨型石胎泥塑彌勒佛，氣勢恢宏，庄严肅穆；小者有幾釐米高的影塑千佛。這諸多造詣精美的彩塑，身身工藝精湛，神彩栩栩如生，姿態婀娜。特別是那魏唐時的許多佳作，被人們譽稱東方的蒙娜麗莎。通過這些古代遺存下來的珍稀佳作，可以瞭解中國古代的政治、經濟、思想、文化，可以探討中國古代的藝術發展規律。它對於研究中國的雕塑史，是一批不可多得的珍貴史料。然而，另一方面，它也閃耀著中國勞動人民的卓越智慧和創造才能的光輝。

　　敦煌絹畫，是指公元1900年（清光緒二十六年）五月二十六日敦煌莫高窟藏經洞（今第十七窟）出土的絹本畫和紙本畫，內容極為豐富，有各種經變、佛像、菩薩像、佛教史跡畫、供養人畫像和裝飾圖案畫等類。此外，同時還出土了數萬卷敦煌遺書，它們包括佛教經典、社會文書，經籍史志以及古藏文、梵文、回鶻文、于闐文、蒙古文等。這些遺書遺畫涉獵到社會科學和自然科學的許多領域：如政治、經濟、軍事、历史、地理、民族、民俗、宗教藝術、美學、文學、文字、音樂、舞蹈、書法、建築、體育、醫學、科技、交通、中外貿易、文化交流等等；並處處都顯示著她那博大精深的輝煌。這皆是中華民族文化的精髓，世界文化史上的一朵奇葩，人類文化遺产的稀世之珍，也是中華民族對人類文明的最傑出貢獻。

　　綜上所述，可見《敦煌石窟珍品》一书，既具有一定深度的學術內涵，又具有相當的廣博性；既有嚴謹、准確的學術價值，又有活潑、流暢的可讀性；既是一本綜合了同類圖書的系統、全面、簡明性的著述，又是一部内容丰富、完整，令人賞心悦目，最有代表性和極富觀賞价值、石窟研究价值的精美圖冊。

北凉篇
Northern Liang (421-439A.D.)

1. 第 272 窟　西壁南側　供養菩薩

Attendant bodhisattvas / Southern side of the West wall / Cave 272

Originally constructed during the Period of Sixteen States, this cave was restored during the Period of Five Dynasties. In total, there are 20 attendant bodhisattvas located in four lines on the southern side of the West Wall. These series of bodhisattvas bare their upper parts of the body and are dressed in heavenly costume and a silk towel. Some of them sit on the ground, others squat on heels, demonstrating varying gestures and postures with much vivacity, elegance and serenity in expression indeed. It falls into the category of the early remnant grottos in Dunhuang Grottoes.

2. 第 272 窟　西壁龕内北側　脅侍菩薩

Escort bodhisattva/Northern side inside the niche on the West Wall/Cave 272

This painting depicts an escort bodhisattva on the northern side of the main statue inside the niche on the West Wall. With an oval-shaped face, long and thin fingers, he is dressed in ribbons which are floating symmetrically, and a crown which is embellished with

trailing plant. The painting depiction is both fine and minute with strong curves and a dignified and elegan dynamic disposal.

3. 第 275 窟　西壁　交脚彌勒菩薩

Cross-legged Maitreya / West wall / Cave 275

Constructed during the Period of Sixteen States an renovated during the Song Dynasty, the Cross-legge Maitreya depicted in this cave ranks among the bigge Maitreya statues in the existing early-period statues o Mogao Grottoes and. With a height of 3.4m, a cripple right hand and the left hand on the knee making a "Wish echoing Seal", this Maitreya is seated cross-legged betwee twin lions with the palm upward, crowned with three pear and an ornamental necklace with bells, a gem string o the chest, a skirt pleated with folding, mud strips an shallow veins in intaglio. With a solemn, tranquil, sublim and detached look, this Buddha is one of the mos outstanding masterpieces in the early statutes

◀4. 第 272 窟　窟頂　疊澀式藻井
Caisson ceiling with caissons superposed one on another /Ceiling/
Cave 272
This caisson is ornamented with lotuses, flames and apsaras, and
with images of its purlins decorated with images of honeysuckles,
surrounded with heavenly dancers and musicians. Beneath the
fending walls of the palace are images of apsaras and a thousand
Buddha. At the center of the roof of the cave is an enormous
blossoming lotus flower in the form of basso-relievo, with frames
of caissons decorated with Lonicera japonica leaves as well as
four corners painted with flame strips and half-naked apsaras
respectively. Looking upwards from down below, you will feel
that the high, arched and distant huge roof is so limitless and real
to life, as if the scenes of cake-construction and picture drawing
by the ancient artists were here just before your eyes.

5. 第 272 窟　藻井外沿　伎樂與飛天
Heavenly Dancers, musicians and apsaras /Outside the caisson
ceiling / Cave 272
Known also as the "Fragrant Musician God" or grandharvas,
Apsaras are heavenly musician or dancer gods charged with
spreading flowers in the Buddhist heaven. Depicting a part of
apsaras around the caisson ceiling, this picture is integral and
unified in structure. All the figures depicted are never the same
with varying vivid gestures and expressions. The elegant
movement of flying, the elegance of dancing gestures and the
thick and strong lines makes the picture more bold and
unconstrained, capable of rendering you into inebriation.

6. 第275窟　南壁　飛天與供養菩薩
Apsaras and attendant bodhisattvas / South wall / Cave 275
Constructed in the Period of Sixteen Nations, this cave was restored during the Song Dynasty. Apsaras and attendant
bodhisattvas in this plate are one part of the fresco on the south wall. The layout of the Apsaras is both fine and excellent
and bodhisattvas' images are vivified with their gracious gestures.

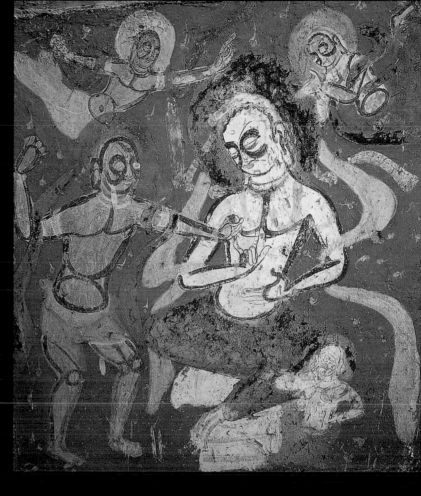

7. 第 268 窟　　西壁龕内　　交脚佛像
Cross-legged Buddha / Niche of west wall / Cave 268
Constructed during the Period of Sixteen States and restored
in Sui and Song dynasties, this cave holds the Cross-legged
Buddha, generally named as Maitreya. This cross-legged
Buddha was the original craft created during the Period of
Sixteen States, but the head of the sculpture was added to during
the Song Dynasty. With a height of 0.76 meter and a kasaya
bare on its right shoulder, this Buddha sits inside the niche
with its legs crossed. On both sides of the niche exterior are
painted attendant bodhisattvas and Apsaras, and on its lintel,
flame design. On the far ends of the exterior sides of the niche
are painted the sole Greek-style columns in Mogao Grottoes.

8. 第 275 窟　　北壁中層　　毗楞竭梨王本生
Jataka of King "Vilenjeli" / Central part, North wall / Cave 275
As one of the early Bunsen story drawings in the Dunhuang
Grottos, King "Vilenjeli" was Sakyamuni's anterior existence.
This drawing depicts the king's eagerness to search for the real
doctrine as well as his willingness to be nailed by Raktasha who,
with a nail in his left hand and a hammer in his right hand, is
about to nail the king's chest. What is most moving of this picture
is that, in face of the threat of Raktasha, the king remained tranquil
and calm, demonstrating his absolute sincerity in his search for
the real doctrine.

9. 第 275 窟　北壁中層　月光王本生

Jataka of King Moonlight / Central part, North wall / Cave 275

Based on a Buddhist story "Moonlight King Grants His Head Due to His Nice Virtue" in the Scripture of the Virtuous and Stupid, this fresco falls into the category of the earliest Bunsen story drawings. Legend has it that the King Moonlight is keen on philanthropic acts and good deeds, thus receiving people's admiration and gratitude. This makes King Pimotts of a small country very jealous, which prompted him to promise a significant reward to the Brahman Raktahsha in return for King Moonlight's head. When Raktahsha asks for the King's head, the King gives him graciously without hesitation and says to the rest of the people: I have given my head for 999 times. Add one more, and this will be the 1000th time. Please let me fulfill my wish of giving my head for 1000 times. With these words, people allowed Raktahsha to chop the King's head away. This painting depicts the scene of the King Moonlight granting his head, where a Tartar is kneeling before King Moonlight and holding a plate with three heads, which shows the king has given his head for 1000 times.

北魏篇

Northern Wei (439-535A.D.)

10. 第254窟　南壁東端　薩埵那太子本生
Jataka of Prince Sudana / East and central part, South wall /
Cave 254
Renovated in Sui Dynasty, this cave features a picture depicting
Prince Sudana sacrificing himself to a hungry tigress. Legend
has it that, one day, the Prince went hunting with his two elder
brothers, where they met a hungry tigress in the mountains that
was going to eat her newborns. In order to save the little tigers
and the tigress, Sudana pierced a bamboo pole into his neck to
make it bleed and jumped off the cliff. The elder brothers
returned home immediately to inform their parents. The parents
went to the valley in a hurry. They cried in tears holding the
corpse of their beloved son in arms, collected his left bones
and erected a pagoda in his memory. This story is touching and
moving in plot, ingenious in composition and compact in layout,
ranking among the masterpieces in early story drawings.

11. 第259窟　北壁龕内　禪定佛像　　　　　　　　▶
Buddha in Dhyana / North niche / Cave 259
Renovated in Song Dynasty, this cave holds a Buddha in
Dhyana, namely, meditation while seated. With a height of 0.92
meter, the Buddha depicted by the picture is dressed in through-
shoulder kasaya with a cone hairstyle, and is seated fully cross-
legged in Dhyana with both hands overlapping making the
Dhyana seal. The Buddha is tranquil and calm in posture in
meditation, with a down-to-earth, free but strict deign, and a
striking but mature coloring technique. It ranks among the most
representative masterpieces of the Dunhuang Statues.

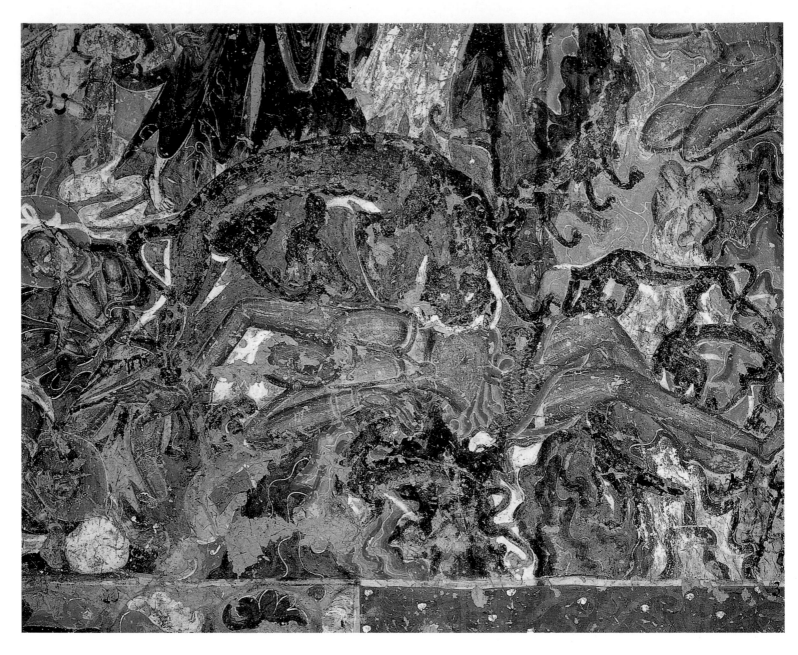

12. 第254窟　南壁東端　薩埵那太子本生（局部）
Jataka of Prince Sudana (Partial) / Central Part, Eastern End of the South Wall / Cave 254
Please refer to the captions of Picture 10, Jataka of Prince Sudana.

13. 第254窟　北壁前部中層　難陀出家
Nanda becoming a monk / Middle upper part, North wall / Cave 254
This picture depicts a vivid story on Nanda's becoming a monk. Legend has it that Nanda is Sakyamuni's younger half-brother who has a nice-looking wife. Sakyamuni orders him to have the tonsure and to be a Pravrajana (monk), but Nanda, madly clinging to his wife, cannot get away from his missing for his wife. One day, Nanda takes advantage of an occasion to go back home, only to be discovered by Sakyamuni, who severely reprimands him and shows him around the Celestial Palace to see heavenly belles (angels), and then leads him to visit the hell to see the most horrible punishments. After the experience, Nanda becomes repentant, shows his remorse and is determined to follow Buddhism, becoming an arhat at long last. In the picture, Nanda is on Buddha's right and lower side. The east and west lower corners depict the attachment between Nanda and his wife. This portrait is rich in content, and is real and lively with an elaborate composition and a compact arrangement, making it the only masterpiece in Dunhuang Grottoes.

14. 第 257 窟　窟頂　平棋圖案
Pattern of caisson ceiling / Ceiling / Cave 257
Reconstructed in Song Dynasty, this cave shows a Caisson design, in which "caisson" is vulgarly known as the ceiling of roofs and "pattern" is known as the various drawings on the ornaments of the architectures. This picture is a square design on the southeastern corner of the posterior ceiling of the Cave 257, which is decorated with various strip patterns as side ornaments. On the four corners of the exterior square are painted apsaras, on those of the second square are flames in the form of mountain and at the center, four naked heavenly figures swimming in a lotus pond. This drawing is unique in style and natural in design, unsophisticated and interesting in content. With an air of primitive simplicity, a coarse curve and uneven thickness, it also vividly embodies the features of early Chinese paintings.

15. 第257窟　中心柱上層南向龕　思維菩薩
Buddha in Dhyana (meditation)/Southward
niche, Upper part of the Central column/Cave 257
Generally called Buddha in Dhyana or in
meditation within the category of Buddha in
Dhyana, the half-clothed Maitreya is located in
the southward niche of the upper column of the
central column. With a height of 0.92 meter, the
Buddha is seated with his right foot on his left
knee and a finger of his right hand supporting
his chin, his body a little bent forward looking
downward, showing a meditating posture. It
demonstrates the Buddha's clear-as-sky mind and
freedom from any disturbing thought.

16. 第257窟　西壁南端《九色鹿本生》中　溺人獲救

Drowned Man Saved/ in the "Nine-colored Deer Bunsen" at the Southern end of the Western Wall/ Cave 257

Pictures 16 and 17 are drawn according to the Buddhist Scripture of the Nine-colored Deer, depicting the nine-colored deer saving a drowned person in the river, after which the drowned person expressed his gratitude to the deer king as well as chatted with him. Legend has it that the deer king saved a drowned person from the Ganges River, who vowed not to reveal the traces of the deer king in order to show his gratitude for its life-saving deed. Later, the empress dreamed of the nine-colored deer and desired to obtain its leather for her bedding and its horn for ornament. Therefore, the emperor promised a high reward for people who hunt the deer. The saved person forgot all about his early vow in front of the reward, and led the emperor to hunt for the deer. The nine-colored deer explained to the emperor the whole story, which moved him deeply and led him to ban the hunting of deer. Later on, both the saved person and the empress died of revenge. The picture is in the horizontal form with a total width of 96 centimeters and a total length of 385 centimeters. According to the needs of the contents, the plot of the story develops from the western end to the middle, forming a climax before it ends. This portrait is complete in structure, vivid and novel in design, smooth in curve and harmonious in colors. It falls into the category of the best masterpieces in story drawings during the Northern Wei Dynasty in the Dunhuang Grottos.

17. 第257窟　西壁南端《九色鹿本生》中　鹿與國王

Deer and the King/ in the "Ninc-colored Deer Bunsen" at the
Southern end of the Western Wall/ Cave 257
See the explanation of the plate 16.

18. 第 251 窟　北壁《説法圖》中　雙飛天

Two apsaras / " Buddha preaching the doctrine", North wall / Cave 251

Reconstructed during the Period of Five Dynasties and Qing Dynasty respectively, this cave features two apsaras in the early Mogao Grottoes, who have the upper part of the body naked. In a long piece of cloth and a long skirt, the two apsaras are dancing elegantly with flying long ribbons.

19. 第257窟　北壁前部　飛天
Apsaras / Anterior part, North wall / Cave 257
These series of Apsaras are located at the anterior part of Cave 257, which are
painted with rough, strong and smooth lines. They have varying flying manners,
and their postures are incomparably gracious, fully reflecting the unique art style of
pictures and the surprising creativity of artists during the North Wei Dynasty.

20. 第 263 窟　　南壁　　降魔變

Conquest of Marapapiyas / South wall / Cave 263
Reconstructed during the Period of Five Dynasties and
Western Xia Dynasty respectively, the picture depicts a
scene of Sakyamuni's conquest of Marapapiyas. At the
center of the picture is a Buddha sitting fully cross-legged,
with one hand holding the front of his gown and the other
one pointing at the floor His body is tall and strong, his
appearance calm and composed. Painted on his sides are
Marapapiyas, or ferocious, bizarre-shaped and hideous
devils. This fresco has a strict composition with a prominent
theme. Sakyamuni's calmness and composedness is in
striking contrast to Marapapiyas' tumult and disturbance.

西魏篇

Western Wei (535-556A.D.)

21. 第249窟　窟頂南披　帝釋天妃

Sakra-devanam-Indra Queen (Western Queen-Mother) / South slope at the Cave Ceiling / Cave 249

Originally created during the West Wei Period and reconstructed during the Qing Dynasty, this painting depicts Sakra-devanam-lndra, alias Western Queen-Mother, on her touring way in a phoenix-cart. According to Shanhaijing, or the Classic on Mounts and Seas, she lived in Mounts Kunlun, to the south of Western Sea, on the vicinity of the Moving Sand, behind the Red River and in front of the Black River. Legend has it that she has tiger teeth and leopard tail, apparently a totem of primitive society. In this picture, however, she is painted as a noble lady in a cart drawn by 3 phoenixes, wearing a robe with big sleeves and standing while cupping one hand in the other before chest. There are one banner-holding immortal and another cart-driving immoral on a male-phoenix, Wuhuo (Hercules), an alchemist and an apsaras following the cart, two monstrous animals named Literate Hawk and White Tiger at its rear. The procession is going westward in running clouds. Down below is a scene of yellowish sheep and wild oxen running in the woods joyfully.

22. 第432窟　中心柱東向龕　彩塑一鋪　▶

A group of painted statues / Eastward niche, Central stupa / Cave 432

Reconstructed in Western Xia period, this cave has a number of color statues created during the West Wei and North Zhou Dynasties. The Buddha falls into the category of sitting Buddha, sitting fully cross-legged with hands in preaching posture. He in dressed in kasaya and monk underwear with a small knot. With the aureole decorated with streaks of flames, his gown pleats are in echelon style, and honeysuckles to be incarnated are painted on the niche lintel, while in the upper part of the lintel, there are attendant bodhisattvas in relief. This color statue is rich in color, florid in style and appropriate in the figures' combination in terms of compactness and tightness. It reflects the fact that, even at that time, the human shape and decorative painting have attained a very fine artistic level. What deserves especial attention is the attendant Buddha on both sides of the exterior of the niche, which is made so charming, tranquil and wonderful by the creator. It truly deserves to be called a representative masterpiece of the Dunhuang Grotto Statues.

23. 第249窟　窟頂西披　阿修羅

Asura / West slope, West ceiling / Cave 249

Translated as " non-God", Asura is an evil spirit in the Indian mythology. According to a Buddhist sutra, he was very poor in his previous incarnation, often having to pass a river to cut firewood. One time, he was nearly drowned after falling accidentally into the river. One day, Pratyeka Buddha, metamorphosed into a monk, asked something to eat from him. After the eating, the Buddha threw away his alms bowl, which rolled and disappeared in the air. So, the poor made a wish to become, in his next being, a giant high enough to pass deep water without wetting his knees. Since he had given foods to Pratyeka Buddha, his body really became tall enough to surpass the Mount Sumeru as well as to stand in the sea without wetting his knees. In this picture, the naked Asura is standing in the sea with the sun and the moon in his hands having 4 eyes, 4 arms and a tall body, escorted by two dragons. Behind him are painted Mount Sumera with uhuo and god of wind on its left, and god of thunder and goddess of lightning on its right. On the lower part of the picture are Han style architectures and on upper part palace, in the architectural style west of China.

24. 第249窟　窟頂北披東卜　野猪群
Wild boars / East lower part, North slope Ceiling / Cave 249
This picture depicts a wild female swine leading her whelps in search of food in the Wood. It is simple and fluent in curve lines, vivacious in describing the wild animals and vivid in portraying the lively scene.

25. 第 249 窟　窟頂北披下部　狩獵圖
Scene of hunting / Lower part, North slop, Ceiling / Cave 249

Depicting a true scene of ancient tribesmen living in the wild, this picture shows two hunters riding on horses tracing the hunt while galloping in the wood. The hunter on the left is turning his body and bending the bow readying himself to shoot an arrow on a tiger, while the one on the right is in pursuit of three Mongolian gazelles and ready to throw his lance. The mountain trees are strewn at random in zigzagged shape. The animals are in multiple forms of gesture, the combination of human figures is appropriate in terms of compactness and tightness, the layout is reasonable and the scene intermingles with the movement very well. With some simple touches of brush, the painter described to the fullest extent the ferocity of tiger, the fear of Mongolian gazelles as well as hunters' courage and his motion in riding gallop.

26. 第 285 窟　窟頂東披
Fuxi, Nuwa et al. / East slope, Ceiling / Cave285

Reconstructed in Mid-Tang, Song, Western Xia and Yuan Dynasties, this cave depicts two vajras holding a Moni pearl and blooming lotuses in the central part of east slope of the ceiling. On their sides are figures of Chinese mythology such as Fuxi, Nuwa, Kaiming (tiger of nine heads with human faces), inhuman being, Wuhuo (Hercules) and apsaras, etc. On the lower part are images of woods and mountains, monk houses, emerging and disappearing animals. Inside the monk houses, the monks are sitting in niches in meditation or having a Buddhist life. Out of niches, there are wandering wild animals running in the mountainous forests. Such a scene with wonderful contrast between the moving and the still makes the whole picture lively, vivid and far-reaching in artistic conception.

27. 第249窟　窟頂東披　力士捧摩尼寶珠

Vajras holding the Mani Pearl / East slope, Ceiling / Cave 249
Although statues of this cave were reconstructed in Qing Dynasty, the frescoes remain originals of Western Wei Period. The Mani Pearl is also called "Pearl of Wishes". Popular legend has it that whoever has this pearl will realize all his wishes. This picture shows two strong and robust vajras holding in their winged hands the Mani Pearl and lotuses in blooms. On both sides are images of apraras and red birds. In the lower

part are images of Tartars and Wuhuo acting various plays, a snake coupling with a tortoise to form Xuanwu (God of the North) and Kaiming (a heavenly animal in from of a tiger having nine heads with human faces), etc. This painting is strict in painting style, organized in terms of compactness and tightness in the picture layout, zigzagged in height and combined in motion and stillness, thus forming a legendary masterpiece in godly pictures.

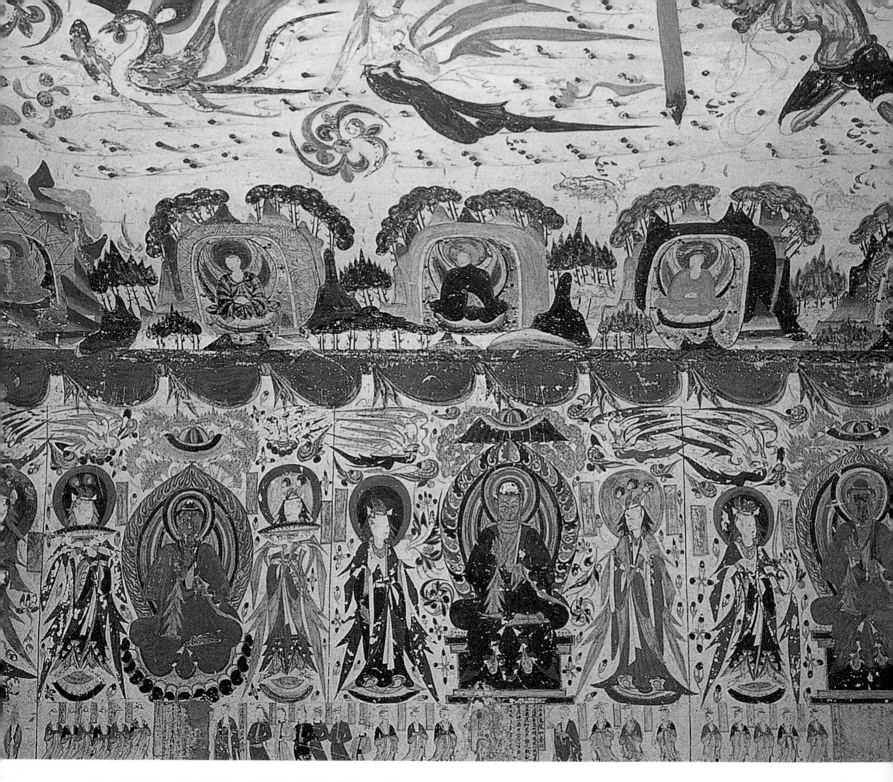

28. 第285窟　北壁上層　説法圖二鋪(七佛之五、六)
Buddha preaching the doctrine (the 5th and 6th of Seven Buddhas) / Upper part, North wall / Cave 285
Depicted in the paining are Kanakamuni Buddha (the 5th) and Kasyapa Buddha (the 6th) counting from the east. The two Buddhas are sitting straight in the middle and looking downward, with smiling faces and their hands showing "fearless" and "granting wishes" gestures. Above the two Buddha are painted images of apsaras who are dancing elegantly on the left and right sides of the baldachin. On the east and west sides of the Buddhas are paintings of two bodhisattvas in slender and comely shape. Under the seats of the two Buddhas is a votum text written with donators' names on both sides of the text. Male donators' names are on the right while female donators' names on the left side. According to the original text under the Buddha seats, the cave was built in 538 AD (the 4th Year of Da Tong), which is the earliest date discovered in this cave.

北周篇

Northern Zhou (557-581A.D.)

29. 第296窟　窟頂北披西段　微妙再嫁梵志

Weimiao's Remarriage to brahmacarins / West part, North Slope, Ceiling/ Cave 296

Reconstructed during the Period of Five Dynasties and Qing Dynasty respectively, this cave paints part of the moving scene of Weimiao's remarriage to brahmacarins, which is based on a story describing the vicissitudes and karma of Nun Weimiao who receives punishment for her sins in her previous life. It is painted in reference to "Sutra of Sages and Sillies vol.3: Bhiksuni Weimiao, 16". Legend has it that, on the night when a son was born to Weimiao, the tipsy husband came back home, cooked the baby and forced Weimiao to eat the baby. Weimiao had no choice but to leave the family. On the road, she met an old man who went to the graveyard where his newly dead wife was buried. The two miserables got married, but the new husband died shortly after their marriage. Weimiao was buried as a sacrifice, but later rescued when bandits robbed the tomb. Weimiao was compelled by force to marry a bandit but he was later caught and put to death, and as a result Weimiao was once again buried as a sacrifice. This time, wolves unearthed her. At last, the painting depicts her meeting Buddha, took the tonsure and became a bhiksuni. This painting is rich in content, flexural, vivid and bleak in plot. The author, through the sad experiences of Weimiao, manages to reveal how previous life sins such as Weimiao's killing a baby in her previous life deserve punishment in a new round of life. It is a representative masterpiece of Dunhuang karma story pictures.

30. 第428窟　東壁南側　薩埵那太子本生

Jataka of Prince Sudana / South part, East wall / Cave 428
Reconstructed during the Period of Five Dynasties, this cave depicts the same story as the one in cave 254 of Northern Wei Dynasty but with a different painting style. The picture is divided by the author into 3 equal parts superposed one on another, forming a complete picture-story in a horizontal painting with the historical technique of "Man bigger than the mount, while the water would not submerge the figures" to stress the figures and the plot. The plots depicted show a hungry tigress, how Sudana sticks his neck to let it bleed and jumps down from the cliff and how two brothers return to the palace to ask the King to collect the left bones and erects a stupa in memory of Sudana, etc. Each plot is dispersed with mountains, tress and houses, forming a natural story serial strip with compact interconnection. The mountains, stones, trees and woods as well as human and animals in the picture are presented right before our eyes, making us feel the charitable deed of the prince to be both

31. 第428窟　南壁　飛天與菩薩

Apsaras and bodhisattvas / South wall / Cave 428

Four semi-naked apsaras are painted on the upper part of this picture, with two of them playing pipa and Konghou (Chinese harp) and the other two dancing. On the lower part are four attendant bodhisattvas, with one of them wearing oblique underwear and holding a sanitary vase. The other three, semi-naked, are dressed in Persian trousers with kneecaps and long towels touching the earth. Although their postures are similar to each other, yet their arms and hands have different gestures.

32. 第432窟　中心柱東向面龕外南側　脅侍菩薩　▶

Escort Buddha / South of the niche exterior, Eastern Part of the Central stupa / Cave 432

This cave was reconstructed during the West Xia Period. The Escort Buddha was created during the West Wei and North Zhou Dynasties with a height of 1.22 meters. One hand of the Buddha is on the chest, while the other droops. Dressed in a long shirt, the Buddha has a long towel on him, smiling with eyes looking down, showing a joyful expression on his face. His cheeks are chubby, his figure is slender, his pose is handsome, and his color is exuberant and bright, demonstrating the aesthetic fashion in the West Wei and North Zhou Dynasties. This painting is also called one of the typical masterpieces of the Dunhuang Grotto color statues.

33. 第428窟　東壁北側　須達拿太子本生（局部）

Jataka of Prince Sudana (detail) / North part, East wall / Cave 428

The Jataka of Prince Sudana is one of the Jataka stories and is based on the Buddhist work Jataka of Prince Sudana Scripture translated by the saints during the West Jin Dynasty. The story, as told by Mr. Fan Jinshi, Director of the Dunhuang Research Institute, goes like this: "Prince Sudana is a benevolent person who answers all requests of the unfavored. A hostile country bribed Brahman Raktahsha to beg for the invincible white elephant from the Prince and the Prince gave the elephant to Brahman ungrudgingly. Upon learning of the news, the furious King dispelled the Prince from his country. On his road in exile, he brought his sons and wife with him, but decided to give away all his belongings, including horse, cart and clothing to the following Brahman Raktahsha. After painstaking efforts, he finally lived a reclusive live in the remote mountains, cultivating himself according to the Buddhist doctrines. But later, the Brahman Raktahsha came again to beg for his two sons, whom Prince Sudana tied up and handed over to Brahman Raktahsha by taking advantage of his wife's absence. When the Brahman sold the two sons on the market of his home country, the king came, redeemed the two sons, and decided to welcome the Prince back home again." The whole painting is divided into three levels depicting more than 50 scenes, illustrating in detail the whole process of the Prince' benevolent deeds. The picture is compact and strict in layout, adept and sophisticated in techniques, and rich in content and description. The vivid and sinuous plot makes people feel as if they were placed at the spot where the story unfolds.

34. 第290窟　中心柱東向面上方　飛天
Apsaras/Upper Position, East Side, Central stupa/Cave 290
Reconstructed in Song Dynasty, the cave depicts Apsaras flying freely face to face around them in the blue sky dotted with budding flowers, not only rendering the whole picture more balanced, but making the atmosphere more bustling as well. Lines used in this painting are simple and clear; colors strong and deep. Apsaras of this kind are rarely seen in Dunhuang Grottoes.

35. 第428窟　前室窟頂　人字披圖案　　　▶
Patterns of Lonicera japonica/Ceiling of Lobby/Cave 428
Patterns of Lonicera japonica refer to human-shaped designs. During the period of Northern Dynasty of Dunhuang Grottos, such designed were often used to decorate the front and rear sides of the ceiling. In the picture are painted crossbeams, sandalwood pieces, rafter and so on. Some rafters are decorated with colorful lonicera japonica, lotuses and auspicious animals. The picture above shows the Patterns of Lonicera japonica at the ceiling of the lobby, which ranks the best in the Dunhuang Grottos. The rafters in the designs are decorated with lotuses, lonicera japonica, and the flowering shrubs are also dotted with running deer, flying birds and playing monkeys, forming a really colorful, magnificent and dynamic scene.

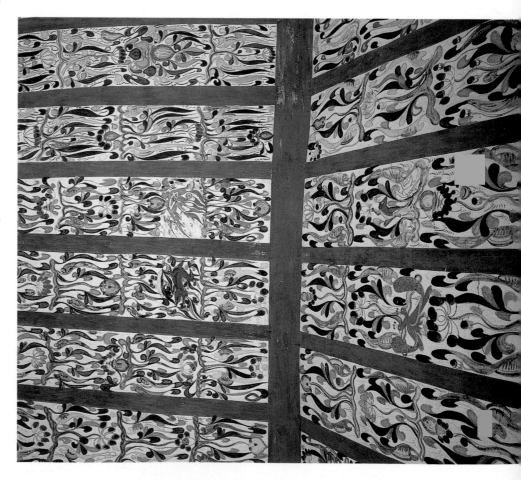

隋代篇

Sui Dynasty (581-618A.D.)

36. 第 305 窟　北壁下部　供養人
Donators / Lower part, North wall / Cave 305
Donators refer to cave masters or merit granters who contributed or raised funds to construct the cave. In Dunhuang Grottoes, the votum text is generally written in the middle with donators on the right and female donators on the left, and two rows are both led by a bhiksuni. In this fresco, however, donators are not identical to those of the other caves at all, and female donators follow donators, whose cause still needs elaboration.

37. 第 419 窟　西壁龕内　彩塑一鋪　▶
A group of painted statues/Interior Niche, west wall/Cave 419
Reconstructed in Western Xia Dynasty, this group has a Buddha sitting at its center with 2 disciples and 2 bodhisattvas on both sides inside the main niche on the West Wall. The Buddha has his right hand raised making a "fearless posture". Dressed in a kasaya with trellis design, his body shape is chubby. His disciple Ananda is intelligent and full of childishness, while Kasyapa, old and emaciated, is lucid and has a frank and open personality. Escort bodhisattvas seem healthy, pretty and well proportionate

38. 第 305 窟　窟頂南披　西王母（帝釋天妃）
Western Queen-Mother (Sakra-devanam-Indra Queen) / South slope, Ceiling / Cave 305
Created in the 5th year of Kaihuang, the Sui Dynasty (585 AD) and reconstructed during the Period of Five Dynasties and Qing Dynasty respectively, this cave depicts the West Queen-Mother flying amid the colorful clouds, riding on a cart dotted with flying banners and flags, drawn westward by 4 phoenixes under the guidance of an immortal driver with angels as vanguards, heavenly animals as escorts and apsaras following the procession. This painting is deeper in coloring but not ungracious, fine in artistic craft but not stagnant, exquisite but not excessive, making itself a top artistic piece in the godly pictures during the Sui Dynasty Period.

39. 第419窟　西壁龕内南側　脅侍菩薩與弟子阿難
Escort bodhisattva and Disciple Ananda / South side, Niche Interior, West wall / Cave 419
Reconstructed during the West Xia Dynasty, the cave holds two statues, one being an escort bodhisattva and the other being disciple Ananda. With a height of 1.81 meters, the bodhisattva is holding a willow branch in the left hand and a sanitary vase in the right one, showing nice facial shape and gracious posture. With a height of 1.65 meters, the disciple Ananda holds an earth bowl in his hand and looks very boyish and handsome. Being the Buddha's close escorts, but of different Buddhist credentials, their shapes are distinguished from the Buddha. Thus, the bodhisattva's statue is generally taller than the disciple's shape.

40. 第419窟　西壁龕内北側　脅侍菩薩與弟子迦葉
Escort bodhisattva and Disciple Kasyapa / North side, Niche Interior, west wall / Cave 419
With a height of 1.81 meters, the bodhisattva is holding a willow branch in the left hand and a sanitary vase in the right hand. His face is severe with clear contour but graceful expressions. Kasyapa, 1.65 m tall, is holding an earth bowl in one hand, with the other hand clutching into a fist before his haggard chest. The bearing of the figures in this picture is lifelike and fine, and its colors simple and elegant. It is also a typical masterpiece of Dunhuang Grotto Color Statues.

41. 第 427 窟　中心柱西向龕　弟子阿難
Disciple Ananda / Westward niche, Central stupa/ Cave 427
Reconstructed in Song Dynasty, the cave depicts Ananda, one of ten disciples of Sakyamuni. With a height of 1.67 meters, he has a comely face, simple clothing and modest dresses, standing respectfully on Sakyamuni's right side with joint palms, listening attentively to Buddha's preaching.

42. 第 420 窟　窟頂東披　西域商隊
A merchant caravan in Western Countries / East slope, Ceiling / Cave 420
Reconstructed in Song and Western Xia dynasties, this cave holds paintings depicting a part of the story in " the Fourth Section of the History of Bodhisattva Avalokitesvara-Saddharma Pundarika Sutra". Bodhisattva Avalokitesvara-Saddharma Pundarika Sutra refers to the Chinese Buddha of Kwan-Yin. These paintings mainly describe the various scenes showing how Bodhisattva Avalokitesvara-Saddharma Pundarika Sutra saved people from disaster and revealed himself to release their souls from purgatory. This painting constitutes one part of the story, depicting the merchant caravan leads hordes of camels fully loaded with merchandise over lofty and precipitous peaks through all kinds of vicissitudes. But however remote, hard and arduous the whole journey was, or even when they encountered bandits, according to the story, merchants would murmur the name of Bodhisattva Avalokitesvara-Saddharma Pundarika Sutra to avoid all kinds of dangers. The ancient artists based their creativity on the contents of the Scripture and drew these interesting and vivid pictures, such as the merchants praying in temples on their journey, feeding medicine to their draught animals, or an animal falling on a mountain slope.... Since Dunhuang was at that time a universally known communication center on the Silk Road and the only road for merchant traffic, the artist painted the breathtaking scenes of hard voyage, dangerous passages based on the people and animals familiar to us in the real life. In this way, we are able to see the elegant demeanor of the historical Silk Road from this wall painting.

43. 第420窟　南向龕　彩塑一鋪
A group of painted statues / Southward niche / Cave 420

Shown above are the statues in the southward niche of this cave, which contains a Buddha and two bodhisattvas. The Buddha, seated fully cross-legged on a colored lion pedestal and preaching, is severe, solemn and has a kasaya with trellis. The two Bodhisattvas on his left and right sides are comely and gracious with shapely appearance with one hand holding a willow twig and the other holding a sanitary vase, looking natural and authentic with clear-cut facial curves as well as brow, nose, lower cheek and smooth transitions. The technique of handling clothing is simple and the design style is corpulent with sumptuous and varied colors. The artistic creation blending molding and painting into an integrated whole by the ancient artists has contributed outstandingly to the circle of art and handicrafts.

44. 第420窟　西壁龕内北側　脅侍菩薩
Attending Bodhisattvas / North side, Niche Interior, West Wall / Cave 420

As shown in the picture, the Attending Bodhisattva is holding a sanitary vase in his right hand and putting his left hand in front of his breast, standing solemnly and gracefully on a lotus pedestal with a round face. The technique of handling clothing is simple and the design style is exquisite with fresh and gracious colors. It ranks among one of the most excellent sculptures of Sui Dynasty in Dunhuang Grottos.

66

45. 第420窟　西壁龕口南側　脅侍菩薩
Escort bodhisattva / South Side, Niche
Entrance, West Wall / Cave 420
Please refer to the captions below picture
44, Cave 420.

46. 第420窟　西壁龕口北側　脅侍菩薩
Escort bodhisattva / North Side, Niche
Entrance, West Wall / Cave 420
Please refer to the captions below picture
44, Cave 420.

47. 第427窟　中心柱南向龕　弟子迦葉
Disciple Kasyapa / Southward niche,
Central stupa / Cave 427
The Kasyapa shown in the picture stands
on Buddha's left side piously, respectfully
and submissively with a thin figure,
joining hand palms and practicing a
Buddhist monk's etiquette. His look is
haggard with flaccid skin and wrinkly
face. But his superciliary ridge, temples
and cheeks have clear contours, his Apple
of Adam is protruding and his eyesight
is fiery, demonstrating his elegant
demeanor with much self-confidence.

初唐篇

Early Tang (618-712A.D.)

70

48. 第 57 窟　南壁中央　説法圖

Buddha preaching the doctrine / Central part, South wall / Cave 57

Reconstructed in Late Tang Dynasty, this picture is just as what was pointed out by Mr. Fan Jinshi, Director of Dunhuang Research Institute --- "paintings showing Buddhas preaching doctrine usually are structured with the Buddha in the foreground, with the attendant Bodhisattva, disciples, doctrine protectors and preaching listeners on the two sides, and with simple baldachin, woods or lotus pond in the background. Hence it is difficult to judge from the picture which Buddha is preaching which doctrine to which disciples in what place at what time. Therefore frescos depicting such themes are generalized as 'Doctrine-preaching Buddha Pictures'." However, this painting is obviously an exception. As shown in this picture, the Maitreya Buddha is seated on a double-lion pedestal under a baldachin between two trees. On his left is Bodhisattva Avalokitesvara, and on his right Bodhisattva Mahasthamahratpa. These three Buddhas are called "Three Saints of the West". On both sides are Kasyapa, Ananda and 8 other bodhisattvas (ten disciples in all), before them are 2 lions and 2 vajras as escorts and dharmapalas (doctrine protectors). Flying in the air are apsaras spreading flowers. This picture has fluent lines, strict and fine layout and rich, beautiful, light and gracious colors, falling into the category of the most excellent and precious masterpieces of the Early Tang Dysnasty.

49. 第 57 窟　南壁中央《説法圖》東側　觀音菩薩 ▶

Bodhisattva Avalokitesvara / East part of the " Doctrine-preaching Buddha", South wall / Cave 57

The Bodhisattva Avalokitesvara in this picture is the most representative and prestigious masterpiece depicting his image in Tang Dynasty, winning itself the title of "Beauty". Due to its beauty, this cave is also called the "beauty Cave" by tourists from home and abroad. The Bodhisattva in the picture has a beautiful and gracious face with moist and smooth skin, elegant and gracious posture, and deep nut gracious coloring. The depiction is delicate nut not stagnant, fine but not excessive. Especially the curve lines on his shawl and skirt are made minute and decorated with various lacework slots. It is not only pleasing to both the eyes and the mind, but shows the sense of beauty appreciated by the people in early Tang Dynasty as well.

◀ 50. 第57窟　北壁中央　説法圖
Buddha preaching the doctrine / Central
part, North wall / Cave 57
Maitreya Buddha at the center of this picture
is sitting on the lotus pedestal under the
baldachin and the bodhi tree. On Both sides
are Bodhisattvas Avalokitesvara and
Mahas-thamahratpa as well as Ananda and
Kasyapa standing piously. On the surface
of Saint Pond, red lotuses are blooming.
Beside the green bodhidruma (bodhi tree)
apsaras are flying and spreading flowers.
This painting is well preserved, delicate in
the painting style and graceful in the
constitution manner.

51. 第57窟　北壁中央《説法圖》右側
大勢至菩薩
Mahasthamahratpa Bodhisattva / Left Side
of the " Doctrine-preaching Buddha", North
wall / Cave 57
This Bodhisattva is plumpy in imag,
gracious in manner, comely and elegant in
appearance, holding flowers standing in the
heavenly pond with blooming lotus flowers.

52. 第71窟　北壁《阿彌陀經變》中　思維菩薩
Buddha in Dhyana (meditation) / Detail of Episode of Maitreya
Sutra, North wall / Cave 71
Constructed in early Tang Dynasty, this cave shows four
bodhisattvas in Dhyana beneath the pedestal of the Buddha,
who have gracious faces with the heads a little bit bent forward.
Some of them have a hand supporting their chin; some have
two joint hand palms; others, left arm akimbo. Under their long
and dark black eyebrows are their fixed and flashing eyes with
solemn and tranquil views as if they have come to realize the
true essence of the Buddhism. This fresco opens out the mystical
mental realm of the bodhisattvas in a vivid manner.

53. 第71窟　北壁　思維菩薩與供養菩薩
Bodhisattvas in Dhyana and attending bodhisattvas/North wall/Cave 71
This cave depicts two bodhisattvas beneath the pedestal of the Buddha
on the North Wall of Cave 71, one being a bodhisattva in Dhyana, the
other being a kneeling attendant bodhisattva. The former, seated fully
cross-legged, is in meditation with his right hand on the knee, and the
left one supporting the cheek. He looks at the immense air with a
smile difficult to ascertain. The attendant bodhisattva kneeling a la
Tartars displays only his back with his head slightly turned to show
the silhouette. His left hand is holding a plate of flowers at the height
of his shoulders. This fresco is delicate in depiction, unique in
conception and vivid in image. It is the most exquisite in all bodhisattva
portraits in terms of posture among all such preserved portraits in
Dunhuang Grottos.

54. 第 220 窟　南壁《阿彌陀净土變》中　舞樂圖

Musician-Dancers-Episode of Maitreya Sukhavati (Paradise)/
South wall / Cave 220
Reconstructed during the middle and late Tang Dynasty periods, the Period of Five Dynasties and Qing Dynasty respectively, this fresco is the complete illustration of musicians and dancers of Sukhavati (western paradise) painted in the 16th year of Zhenguan, Tang Dynasty (642). The Maitreya Sukhavati (Paradise) Episode is also called Western Episode, falling into the category of Dunhuang Buddhist Episode Portraits. Shown in this picture are two dancers with crown decorated with precious stones, bracelets mounted with bells, holding long ribbons, and having an oblique celestial dress and a red and transparent silk skirt. They dance elegantly face to face on a luxurious rug. According to the history books of Tang Dynasty, it was called the "Huxuan Dance". On both sides of this dance, there are respectively 8 musicians sitting on rugs with various patterns and playing ancient harp, pipa, vertical flute, clappers, Fangxiang, 25 stringed zither, triton, waist drum, and other Sino-occidental musical instruments. It is a re-appearance of the grand occasion of dancing and music in the imperial court at the time and a rare historical document on Chinese music, depicting a magnificent and grand scene.

第 220 窟　　南壁　　一佛二菩薩
One Buddha and Two Bodhisattvas/
South Wall/ Cave 220
The Maitreya Buddha as shown in this
picture is dressed in through kasaya,
sitting on the lotus pedestal in the
heavenly pond under the bodhi tree. The
pond is full of grebe water and the divine
children are playing in the water, while
the Bodhisattva Avalokitesvara and the
Mahasthamahratpa Bodhisattva are
standing graciously on both sides. They
are all masters of the Western Elysium,
called collectively as the "Three Saints
in the West". This portrait is rich in
color, elegant in human figure, smooth
and natural in curve lines. It is a rare
precious masterpiece in the Early Tang
Dynasty.

58. 第 220 窟 北壁《藥師净土變》東側
    樂 隊
    Orchestra / East part, Episode of
    " Medicine-Buddha Sutra" on North
    Wall / Cave 220
    Depicted in this portrait is an orchestra
    consisting of 13 musicians playing all
    kinds of musical instruments: 25
    stringed zither, Chinese flute, vertical
    flute, Fang Xiang, horizontal flute,
    waist drum, clappers, etc. Although of
    different skin colors, these musicians
    are all concentrated on playing, and all
    have different gestures playing their
    instruments in a harmonious relation
    between the principle and the
    subordinate, the solo and the
    concerto.... It is an illustration of the
    real court concert at the time.

59. 第220窟　東壁南側　維摩詰
Vimalakirti / South part, East Wall / Cave 220
Shown in the picture is a portrait of Vimalakirt in the upper south part of east wall, who holds a feather fan and sits on the bed. His body pitches forward a little with eyebrows crossed; but his eyes are bright and radiate an air of confidence and thoughtfulness. The author got the whole artwork done without any letup with smooth and strong strokes, making people feel as if " The moustache and hair on the temples were flying several feet away and the root of the hair were out of the flesh, with excesses of strength."

60. 第 220 窟　東壁北側　帝王圖

The Emperor's Portrait / North Part, East Wall / Cave 220
Painted in the 15th Year of Zhengguan of Tang Dynasty
(642AD), this picture is one part of the Vimalakirt Episode.
It mainly depicts the Emperor, the ministers, the princes
and officials paying a visit to somebody as described by
the Buddhist scripture " Convenient Rank". The Emperor
in the picture is tall and fat, wearing a formal top hat
decorated with jade strings as well as cyan clothes. With a
air of superiority, magnificence and solemnity, he opened
his arms and marched forward with his head a bit raised
under the escort of the officials. This portrait is smooth and
strong in curve lines, voluptuous and luxuriant in coloring,
mild and fine in areola, reflecting the author's fluent and
superb portraying techniques.

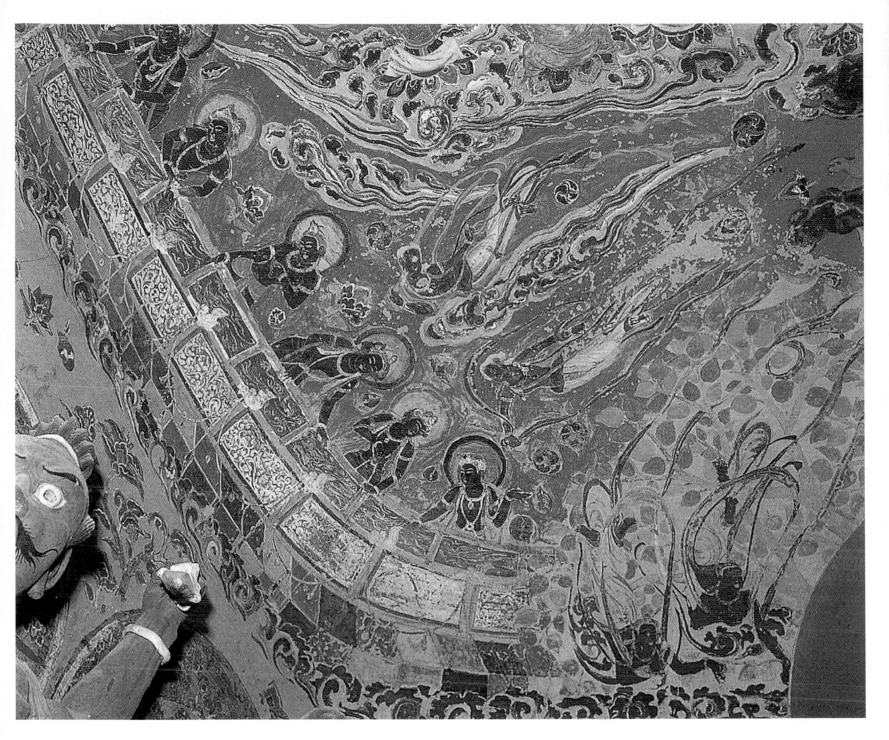

61. 第 321 窟　　西壁龕頂南側　　菩薩赴會
Bodhisattvas participating an assembly / South part above
the niche, West wall / Cave 321
Reconstructed in the Period of Five Dynasties and Qing
Dynasty respectively, this cave depicts Apsaras flying freely
in the background of a blue sky. Six bodhisattvas with
graceful carriage join the assembly by riding on colorful
clouds and lean on the pavilion balustrade in the celestial
palace, looking downward as to contemplate the common
secular life. They point, talk and discuss in a joyful and
harmonious air full of interest.

63. 第322窟 東壁門上方《説法圖》中
菩 薩
Bodhisattva / Upper part East wall
above the gate / Cave 322
This cave features the bodhisattva in
the "Preaching Doctrine under a
Tree" in the upper part of the East
Wall above the gate. The bodhisattva
is sitting fully cross-legged in a lotus
flower, with his head a little declined,
his eyes half-closed looking
downward, a hand holding flowers
and the other one a ribbon. He looks
calm and indifferent to the outside
world. This portrait is refined and
strict in designing technique, mild
and suave in touches, mild in coloring
and elegant in interest.

62. 第322窟　南壁　説法圖
Doctrine preaching / South wall / Cave 322
Reconstructed in the Period of Five Dynasties, this fresco is called
"Maitreya Preaching the Doctrine", in which Maitreya, the main Buddha
in it, sits half-cross-legged under the bodhidruma canopy, with bodhisattvas
standing on both sides. Bodhisattvas have elegant postures with simple
dress and adornment of different colors, rich but not excessively brilliant.
This picture falls into the category of simple and elegant portraying style
in early Tang Dynasty Period.

64. 第 322 窟
西壁龕内北側
天王與菩薩
Bodhisattvas and the
Lokapala / North internal
side of the niche near West /
Cave 322
Please refer to the caption to
Picture No. 65, "A group of
painted statutes".

65. 第 322 窟　西壁龕内南側　彩塑一鋪

A group of painted statutes / south internal side of the niche near West wall /Cave 322

This niche holds 7 statues, but the photo shows only four with Sakyamuni at the center and his disciple Ananda, bodhisattvas and lokapala on the southern side. Sakyamuni, 1.76 meter tall, with a round forehead and high nose ridge, is seated seriously in fully cross-legged form on his lotus seat with a kasaya. He looks solemn and serious. Ananda, 1.60 meter tall, in a thrifty and simple dress, stands piously and respectfully on the Buddha's side. The bodhisattva, 1.60 meter tall and dressed in a heavenly consume, with his left hand raised, and is seated with a calm expression on the lotus seat. With damaged hands, the Kapala has a long shawl, a grey cuirass and boots high enough to protect his legs. One of his feet is put on an earth deity, which makes him look very powerful and commanding.

66. 第 329 窟　　窟頂　　蓮花飛天藻井
Caisson ceiling with lotuses and apsaras / Ceiling / Cave 329
Caisson ceiling with lotuses and apsaras is one kind of caisson
designs. The picture shown in Cave 329 is one of the paintings
completed in early Tang Dynasty featuring lotus and apsaras'
images. The painting is well done, with well-structured lines
and strokes with interwoven compactness and tightness. The
whole picture is very exuberant in color and lively in
atmosphere, especially the four handsome apsaras who dance
gracefully against the background of blue sky with their
ribbons waving lively together with the white clouds. This
fresco is renowned as a typical masterpiece of caisson designs
in early Tang Dynasty.

67. 第 329 窟　　東壁南側　　女供養人　　▶
Donatress / South part of East wall / Cave 329
Painted in early Tang Dynasty and reconstructed during the Period of
Five Dynasties and Qing Dynasty respectively, this painting, located
below the picture "Preaching doctrine" on the south side of east wall,
depicts the image of a donatress. The donatress is very chubby but looks
dignified and calm. With tied up hair, she is wearing a coat with narrow
sleeves and round collar, a long skirt and a transparent shawl on her
shoulders. She is sitting on a rug and looking forward, holding a lotus in
her hand. This painting successfully created the image of a gracious
lady with high social status in early Tang Dynasty through a realistic
approach. It is a rare masterpieces of donatresses succeeding in revealing
to us the internal thoughts of noble ladies in Dunhuang Grottoes.

68. 第329窟　西壁龕頂南側　夜半逾城

Crossing the city wall in midnight / South Part of West Wall,
Niche Ceiling / Cave 329

The picture depicts a scene of Buddhist stories. Having witnessed
the pains in human world such as birth, aging, sickness and death,
Prince Siddhartha,19 years old, decides to leave the family to
practice the Buddhism. One midnight, with a crown on his head,
he crosses the royal city wall on a white horse back followed by
his cart-driver holding a horsetail whisk. The picture depicts the
crowned prince galloping through the clouds. Before the horse is
an apsaras riding on a tiger playing the role of their guild. After
the horse are celestial girls and vajras as their guards and escorts.
Apsaras are flying freely in colorful clouds and decorate the scene
in festoons and in an auspicious, colorful and magnificent air. The
whole picture is filled with flowery colors, which reproduces the
moving scene of the Buddha's decision to dedicate himself to the
Buddhist religion.

69. 第321窟　東壁北側　十一面觀音
Eleven-faced Bodhisattva Avalokitesvara / Northern Side of the Eastern Wall / Cave 321
The Eleven-faced Bodhisattva Avalokitesvara is also called Grand Light Thrown All over the World Bodhisattva Avalokitesvara, as one of the six Bodhisattva Avalokitesvaras. This Bodhisattva Avalokitesvara has eleven faces and six hands, is dressed in transparent shirt, and holds one sanitary vase on one hand, and a willow twig on the other. Standing on the lotus pedestal under the two trees with a solemn appearance, he is escorted by two attending Bodhisattvas with charming and slender outlook. This picture is preserved well with symmetrical and strict layout. It is smooth and fine in strokes, mild in curve lines but showing rigidity at the same time, curved and strong in style, as well as sophisticated and complicated in techniques. This portrait is indeed one of the famous art crafts in Tang Dynasty.

◄

70. 第 220 窟
北壁《藥師經變》西側　伎樂
Heavenly musicians/West of "Episode of Medicine-Buddha Sutra", West wall / Cave 220

The picture depicts the image of a musician in the band of the "Episode of Medicine-Buddha Sutra" on the north wall of the cave, who is holding an instrument with his two hands and playing very attentatively. Judging from the musical instrument he is using, he must be from a coastal place in the south. By depicting the details of the musician such as his appearance, posture and musical instrument, the painter manages to demonstrate the nationality features of the figure in an implicit way. The whole picture is vivid and true to life in terms of human description, cyclical and fluctuant in terms of layout design, elegant in coloring and saint in style.

71. 第 321 窟　西壁龕頂南側　雙飛天
Twin Apsaras/ Southern Side of the Niche Top, West Wall/ Cave 321

According to sutra, the apsaras is the development of "Gandhabba" and "Kimnara". The apsaras, one of eight celestial dragons, often flies in the sky of Buddhist region. Gandhabba is the god of singing in ancient Indian mythology, and he is said to be a very handsome man. Kimnara is the goddess of musical instruments in ancient

►

Indian mythology, and she is the wife of Gandhabba when she is in her female body form. In the picture are two apsaras on the south part of niche ceiling of west wall in Mogao grottoes cave 321 painted in early Tang Dynasty. The apsaras have delicate form, smooth line, and slim figure, which is pleasing to both the eyes and the mind. This painting is one of the best pieces of apsaras in early Tang Dynasty.

72. 第57窟　西壁龕内南側　菩薩
Bodhisattva / South part, West niche / Cave 57

The picture depicts a statue of Bodhisattva to the south of the Buddha statue in cave 57, who is holding a sanitary vase in her right hand and a lotus flower in her left hand. She stands by the side of Buddha with a calm expression. Although the image of this Bodhisattva is not as charming and graceful as those created in middle Tang Dynasty, it nonetheless exhibits a kind of feminine calmness and grace. The reason can partly be attributed to the fact that the statue-making techniques are during the transition from the Sui Dynasty style to that of the Prosperous Period of Tang Dynasty.

盛唐篇

High Tang (712-781A.D.)

73. 第45窟　西壁龕内北側　菩薩（局部）
Bodhisattvas (partial) / North Side, Niche Interior, West wall / Cave 45
This charming and slender Tang Dynasty statue of Bodhisattva is one of the most beautiful and unique in Dunhuang Grotto Statues. With a height of 1.85meters, this graceful bodhisattva has a crown on his tied up hair, a gem string before his chest with a shawl obliquely draped over one shoulder, and an embroidered silk skirt. His skin is fine and smooth. His posture is elegant, charming and delicate, making it a rare treasure that can hardly be obtained.

74. 第45窟　西壁龕内北側 ▶
迦葉·菩薩·天王
Kasyapa, Bodhisattva, Lokapala/North side, Niche Interior, West wall/Cave 45
Built in early Tang Dynasty and reconstructed in middle Tang Dynasty and the Period of Five Dynasties respectively, Cave 45 holds three statues of Kasyapa, Bodhisattva and Lokapala on the north side of the Niche Interior on the West wall. The Kasyapa, 1.75m high, is sophisticated and prudent. With a height of 1.85 meters, the bodhisattva is elegant and brilliant with black eyebrows, and gracious and natural gesture. The lokapala, 1.79m high, is strong and full of power with eyes largely opened and full of fury. Although the three have different characters and identities, yet they form a coherent and uniform entity. The three statues are the most excellent masterpieces in the Prosperous Period of the Tang Dynasty in the Dunhuang Grottos, and are representative works in the colorful statues of the Dunhuang Grottos.

75. 第45窟　南壁西側　商人遇盗圖
Merchants encountering robbers/West part, South wall/Cave 45
The portrait depicts the scenes of robbery encounter in a story
told in "Avalokitesvara Sutra", in which a group of merchants
who are walking in the wild with silk and precious
merchandises encounter three robbers with swords. The

merchants are forced to download their merchandises from
the backs of their donkeys. In the picture, the panic of the
merchants, the yelling of donkeys, the rudeness of the robbers
as well as the wildness of the woods are all well depicted,
which reproduces vividly before our eyes scenes of the
merchants' route on the ancient Silk Road.

76. 第 45 窟　北壁　觀無量壽經變（全）

Aparimitayur Sutra Episode (general view) /North wall/Cave 45
As the abbreviation of the Aparimitayur Sutra Buddha Episode, Aparimitayur Sutra is a classical Buddhist scripture translated from Sanskrit into Chinese in as early as the Period of Three Warring States (originally there were three ones, There is only a book entitled Jiangliangyeshe left behind). This painting takes as its center the images of western Pure Land, and on the two sides are two other joining horizontal images, namely the "Future-Borns Grief " and "Sixteen Views", to form a triptich. In the picture Maitreya is sitting on a lotus seat preaching Buddhist doctrines and on two sides are Bodhisattvas who are listening attentively. Down below are bands playing, showing the prosperous scene of "Western Paradise". The author depicts the kindness and calmness of Buddha, the concentration of Bodhisattvas, the joyfulness of music and dances as well as the magnificence of buildings in a fervent, harmonious and beautiful manner, making people feel the charm of the Western Paradise.

◀ 77. 第23窟　北壁西側　雨中耕作圖
Cultivation in the rain / West part of North wall / Cave 23
Re-painted in Middle Tang and the Period of Five Dynasties
with statues rebuilt in Qing Dynasty, frescoes in this cave
depict the scene of plowing in rain as told in "Medicinal Herb-
Saddharma Pundarika Sutra". This picture unfolds before us
a sky full of nimbuses with a lasting drizzle sufficient for the
lands abundant with crops and of medicinal herbs. Some
farmers are shouldering a load in the rain, while others are
plowing laboriously. A peasant woman is on road to bring
some foods to them. The author depicts the scene of ancient
farmers plowing in the rain laboriously painted with a beauty
of pastoral poetry in a lively and true-to-life manner.

78. 第39窟　西壁龕頂　飛天
Apsaras / Upper part of West wall, niche / Cave 39
Reconstructed during the Period of Five Dynasties, West
Xia Dynasty and Qing Dynasty respectively, this cave
features a picture in which an Apsara with long skirt and
shawl holds flowers and descends from the heaven. The skirts
and shawls are colorful and seem particularly beautiful
against the backdrop of colorful clouds. Although the colors
on the face and body of the apsara have faded, yet his graceful
gesture can still be felt, and the curve lines are also very
smooth and strong. It is one of the most characteristic
paintings of Apsaras in Dunhuang Grottos.

79. 第79窟　西壁龕内　彩塑一鋪
A group of painted statues / West wall, niche / Cave 79
Reconstructed during the Period of Five Dynasties, this cave features a group of painted statues including a Buddha, two disciples and 4 bodhisattvas in the tent-like niche, with two lokapalas on both sides out of the niche. Inside the niche the Buddha is sitting in the middle, with a short forehead and a chubby face and wearing a kasaya with trellis patterns. He is raising his right hand to make a "preaching" posture and appears very calm with a slight smile. The four Bodhisattvas, in comparison, are naked in their upper bodies, with shawls obliquely hung over their shoulders. The two disciples are barefoot and stand piously by the side of the Buddha. The Lokapalas have broad shoulders and strong arms and stand gravely by the two sides. The statues are well preserved, well positioned and brightly colored, symmetrically positioned to each other in layout. The human figures are fleshy in body and delicate in skin. Although they have undergone many repairs, they still relay an air of artistic beauty typical of Tang Dynasty statues.

80. 第130窟　西壁　大佛（局部）　▶
Great Buddha (partial) / West Wall / Cave 130
This cave was originally constructed in the Prosperous Period of Tang Dynasty and rebuilt in the Song Dynasty. The Great Buddha shown in the picture is one of the two great Buddha statues in Mogao Grottos, winning itself the prestige as the Second Largest Buddha, or Southern Great Buddha according to the Mogao Grottos Chronicle. With a height of 26 meters, it was constructed between AD713 and 721, namely around the Ninth Year of Kaiyuan in Tang Dynasty, as a Maitreya Buddha Statue with fully crossed legs. This Buddha has a bearing of tolerant for almost all happenings as well as a grand, magnificent and commanding air.

81. 第 148 窟　東壁南側　觀無量壽經變（全）
Aparimitayur Sutra Episode (general view) / South part,
East wall / Cave 148
This cave was repaired in Late Tang, Western Xia and Qing
Dynasties respectively. Depicted in the picture is the largest
Episode Portraits in the Dunhuang Grottos, with the Western
Pure Land ("Maitreya's Sukhavati") as the center and
"Future-borns Grief" and "Sixteen Views" on both ends of
the fresco.　Buddha Aparinlitayur sits on the central
platform, who is preaching on the lotus seat under

Mahasthamahratpa, as well as their escort bodhisattvas. On
the platform above the water, two dancers are dancing,
accompanied by orchestras on both sides. In the Saint Pond
on the lower part of the picture, children-to-be reborn sit in
lotus flowers and play with one another. In the upper part
of the picture are grandiose and magnificent palaces which
are close resembles of palaces in the Tang Dynasty. This
picture has different themes, with complicate and vivid
intrigues, a fine and delicate description and strong and
luxuriant colors. It provides a good and valuable reference
to the study of Tang Dynasty architectures

女十一娘供養

女十三娘供養

82. 第130窟　　甬道南壁　　都督夫人太原王氏供養像
Governor's wife worshipping the Buddha / South wall, Tunnel / Cave 130
This picture depicts a Governor's wife and her family worshipping Buddha,
with the former looking very dignified, dressed in red skirt and long shawls
dripping to her feet. She stands piously on the flower rug under a canopy. The
caption on the pictures reads "Taiyuan Governor's wife Madam Wang paying
tribute". The lady beside with green long skirts and the lady holding flower and
wearing a yellow long skirt are Madam Wang's two daughters, with the caption
reading "the 11th Lady Wholeheartedly Paying Tribute" and "the 13th Lady
Wholeheartedly Paying Tribute". Nine servants in male costume are standing
behind. Human figures in this picture are very fleshy in appearance, lively and
gracious in expression, bright in colors and clear in design. It is the only most
rare precious artwork in the Dunhuang Grottos.

83. 第172窟　南壁　觀無量壽經變（全）
Aparimitayur Sutra Episode (general view) / South wall / Cave 172

Constructed in Middle Tang Dynasty and reconstructed in Song and Qing Dynasties respectively, this cave features the whole view of the huge Aparimitayur Sutra Episode on the South Wall of the cave. At the center are three palaces complemented by side-halls, turrets, round kiosks of pagoda that form joint through platform bridges. Before the palaces and in the middle are the solemnly preaching Buddha Aparimitayur, who sits under the canopy on the lotus pedestal with kasaya; and the Avalokitesvara and Mahasthamahratpa bodhisattvas who are listening attentively to the preaching. Musicians seated before the palace are playing Buddhist pieces. The bands on both sides are playing in accompaniment. In the green Holy Pond, mandarin ducks swim leisurely among red lotus flowers. The pavilions and palaces hidden behind the green trees and water can especially reflect the implicative and meaningful nature of the portrait. It also makes the whole picture deeper in thoughts' realm and more grandiose in layout.

84. 第172窟　北壁　觀無量壽經變（全）

Aparimitayur Sutra Episode (general view) / North wall / Cave 172
Aparimitayur in this portrait is sitting cross-legged on the central platform in the palace. Though the color painted on his face has faded and some parts have been destroyed, yet his generous and solemn bearing can still be felt. Buddhas, old and young, are listening carefully to the preaching; some are in meditation. Musicians seated before the palace are playing Buddhist pieces; white cranes are crying loudly in the sky; Apsaras are flying in the sky; Mandarin ducks are swimming leisurely among red lotus flowers and green lotus leaves in the treasure pond, and some of children-to-be-reborn are swimming in the pond. Such a unique scene of happy and calm life is filled with the real interest of life in the Buddhist State.

85. 第172窟　　北壁東側
十六觀中　　日想觀

The Sixteen Views (detail): Sun
Meditation / Upper part, East side
of North wall / Cave 172

As the first view of the sixteen
views in the Aparimitayur Sutra
Episode, Sun Medication View
depicts green river water washing
away the deep red rock on the
cliffs. In far west, the sun is
setting, with its rays reddening the
silhouette of the rocks. In nearer
places, trees with few leaves and
fallen foliage can be seen. Under
a secluded cliff, Madam Wei Tixi
is kneeling eastwards with incense
stove in hand, looking at the red
sun gradually being hidden by the
dark clouds. In terms of the
scenery depicted, the picture is
quite sad in theme, but the dim
rays of the setting sun somewhat
breaks the coldness of the whole
portrait.

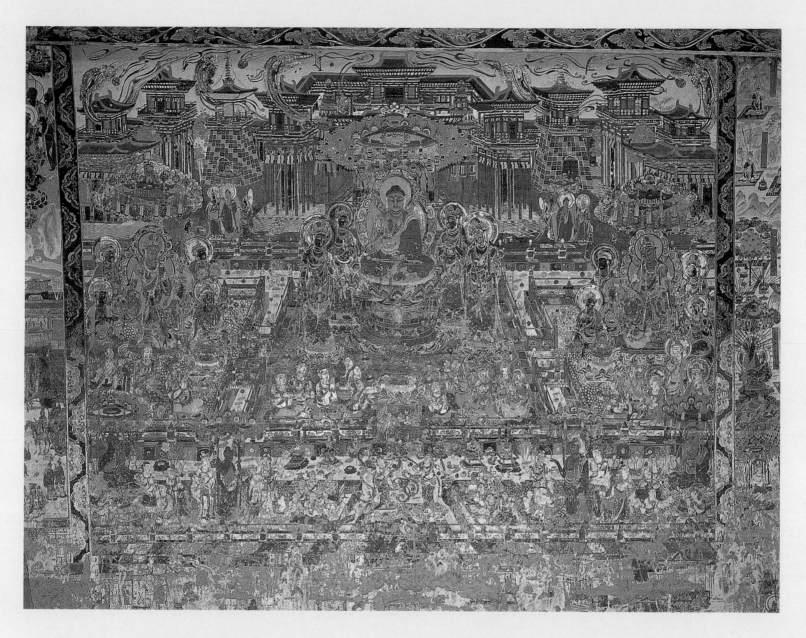

86. 第217窟　北壁　觀無量壽經變（全）
Aparimitayur Sutra Episode (general view)/North wall/Cave 217
Reconstructed in Late Tang Dynasty, the Period of Five Dynasties and Qing Dynasty respectively, this cave features a picture worthy of the title as the most sumptuous of Aparimitayur Sutra Episode pictures. The grandiose architectural constructions in it, the Buddha preaching doctrine on Mount Grdhrah-Ta (Mount Vulture), the attentive bodhisattvas, the musical bands and dancers as well as the graceful apsaras spreading flowers in the sky combine together to exhibit the weird and grandiose scenery in the Western Paradise. This painting is magnificent in theme, deep in strokes, bright and rich in colors as well as rich in royal construction styles. It reproduces the superb painting skills and architectural styles of middle Tang Dynasty.

87. 第 217 窟　北 壁
《觀無量壽經變》東側
坐佛與菩薩
Seated Buddha and Bodhisattvas /
North Wall Below, East of the
"Aparimitayur Sutra Episode" /
Cave 217
This painting describes the Buddha
and Bodhisattva in the Amitayus
paradise as shown in the lower part
of the "Aparimitayur Sutra"
Episode. The Buddha is sitting
cross-legged on the lotus seat in a
very dignified and solemn way.
Since the Buddha has become deep
red, it is also called " Purple Ridden
Golden Body". The Bodhisattva is
very handsome and stands
graciously beside the Buddha
listening to the preaching. The
painting combines both dark and
mild ink lines in a sophisticated and
refined use of technique, making
itself one of the most excellent
works in Tang Dynasty.

88. 第 217 窟　北壁西側　　　▶
《觀無量壽經變》中　阿彌陀佛
Amitoba/North Wall Within the
"Aparimitayur Sutra Episode"/
Cave 217
The Buddha Amitayus in the
picture is looking forward and
seated upright on the lotus seat.
Above is a canopy held by apsaras
and on the two sides are four
attendant bodhisattvas. The
painting is bright in color,
symmetrical in layout, strict in
style, refined in painting,
sophisticated in techniques, fully
reflecting the aesthetic styles in
Tang Dynasty.

89. 第217窟　　南壁西側　　化城喻品

Legend of an illusory city/West side, South wall/Cave 217

Depicted in the portrait is a scene of a legend described in "Saddharma Pundarika Sutra". According to the legend, a group of explorers went in search of a treasure in a remote country under a guide who, in fact, was an immortal. The road was difficult, the land deserted. On the way, they experienced great hardships, fatigue and thrilling scenes, and fell in a hesitation. On this critical occasion, the guide made an illusory city with his magic power, invited them to take a rest in it and encouraged them to continue with their journey. This picture depicts several scenes with the guide at the center right with naked body, bare foot and short skirt, leading the way for the explorers. Behind him are two persons riding the horse following them. There are winding mountains, thick forests and rivers flowing sinuously among them in the picture, giving the whole artwork a strong nationality connotation.

90. 第217窟　西壁龕頂　説法圖（局部）
Doctrine preaching (detail)/Niche ceiling, West wall/Cave 217
What this picture depicts is the scenes of Sakyamuni preaching
the doctrine to the general masses and going back home with

his disciples to see his mother. This picture is well-conceived in
layout, appropriate in handling, accurate and lively in human
figure designs, strong in ink lines and splendid in coloring. It is
the best conserved fresco in terms of colors in Tang Dynasty

◀ 91. 第217窟　西壁龕內北側　比丘
Bhiksu / North part, Niche, West wall / Cave 217
Shown in the picture is a portrait of disciple Bhiksu rarely seen in Tang Dynasty. In an embroidered kasaya, Bhiksu has heavy eyebrows, big eyes, some deep wrinkles and a smile, standing on the lotus platform with both surprise and joy. The painting is deep in coloring, elegant in style and vivid in creating human figures. It truly exhibits the charm of Tang Dynasty.

92. 第320窟　南壁《阿彌陀經變》上部　雙飛天
Two Apsaras / Upper part of " Maitreya Sutra Episode", South wall / Cave 320
Reconstructed in Middle Tang Dynasty, Song and Yuan Dynasties respectively, this cave has earned itself the prestige as "apsaras everywhere" in Dunhuang frescoes.

In this Picture, 4 apsaras are flying in pairs – some are spreading flowers and others are chasing each other in joyful playing. This picture is vivid with detailed descriptions, trying to be perfect in its style. It is strong in strokes, smooth in style and splendid in coloring, ranking among the most divine artworks in Apsaras paintings.

94. 第 328 窟　西壁龕内中央　坐 佛
Seated Buddha / Center of the Niche on the West
Wall / Cave 328
With a height of 2.19 meters, this seated Buddha is sitting
properly and solemnly at the center of the niche on the West

Wall in this cave, appearing very dignified and serious. The
pleats of the Buddha's clothes, head aura, back aura and neck
aura as well as the Buddha seats are all painted with bright
colors by the superb painting masters, which makes the statue
decorated with rich color and gold-like texture.

93. 第 328 窟　西壁龕内佛壇　彩塑一鋪
A group of painted statues / Bodhisattva platform, West niche /
Cave 328
This group of painted statues is originally composed of 9 statues,
but there are now only 8 statues left. The attendant bodhisattva
on the exterior south side was stolen by Warner, USA, in 1924
and is now displayed in Boston Museum. With a height of 2.19
meters, the Buddha sitting properly and solemnly in the middle
is one of best-conserved Tang statues. The Bodhisattvas on both
sides are respectively 1.87m and 1.90m high (seats included).
They sit half cross-legged with a leg hanging down and another
foot put on its knee. This posture is also called "game playing
posture". Their dress and adornments are magnificent and

shaping strict, showing their elegant demeanor and intelligence.
The disciple Amanda, on the south side, is 1.83m high, and has
a pretty face and a high spirit with his hands in sleeves. The
disciple Kasyapa, 1.80m high, has joint hand-palms, and appears
to be calm and humble. The attendant bodhisattva on the north
side of the niche is 1.12 m tall. He kneels sincerely a la Tartare
on the lotus seat and seems to be meditating over something.
The 1-meter-tall Attendant bodhisattvas on the southern and
northern sides out of the niche are also kneeling a la Tartare in
a gentle, quiet, gracious and pious manner. These fine statues
are made with a very high artistic attainment, and are the most
representative masterpieces of Tang statues in Dunhuang
Grottoes of the Tang Dynasty.

95. 第 328 窟　西壁龕内北側
半跏菩薩
Half Cross-legged Bodhisattva /
Northern Part, Niche Interior,
West Wall/ Cave 328
See the explanation of the plate
93: "A group of painted statues".

96. 第 328 窟　西壁龕内北側　▶
半跏菩薩（局部）
Half Cross-legged Bodhisattva
(partial) / Northern Part, Niche
Interior, West Wall / Cave 328
See the explanation of the plate
93: "A group of painted statues".

97. 第328窟　西壁龕内南側　半跏菩薩
Half Cross-legged Bodhisattva / Southern
Part, Niche Interior, West Wall /Cave 328
See the explanation of the plate 93: "A
group of painted statues".

98. 第328窟　西壁龕内北側　▶
迦葉與菩薩
Kasyapa and Bodhisattva / Northern Part,
Niche Interior, West Wall/Cave 328
See the explanation of the plate 93: "A
group of painted statues".

99. 第 328 窟　　西壁龕内南側　　阿難與菩薩
Amanda and Bodhisattva / Southern Part, Niche
Interior, West Wall / Cave 328
See the explanation of the plate 93: "A group
of painted statues".

100. 第 328 窟　　西壁龕内南側　　▶
弟子阿難（局部）
Amanda and Bodhisattva(partial) / Southern
Part, Niche Interior, West Wall / Cave 328
See the explanation of the plate 93: "A group
of painted statues".

103. 第328窟　西壁龕外北側　供養菩薩
Attendant Bodhisattva / Northern Part, Niche
Exterior, West Wall / Cave 328
See the explanation of the plate 93: "A group of
painted statues".

104. 第328窟　西壁龕外南側　供養菩薩
Attendant Bodhisattva / Southern Part, Niche Exterior, West Wall /
Cave 328
Please refer to the caption to Picture No. 93 in Cave 328, "A group
of painted statues" for pictures No.101, 102, 103 and 104.

中唐篇

Middle Tang (781-848A.D.)

105. 第112窟　　南壁東側《觀無量壽經變》中　　反彈琵琶
Playing Pipa Reversely / "Aparimitayur Sutra" Episode,
East part, South wall / Cave 112
Reconstructed in Song Dynasty and Qing Dynasty
respectively, this cave features a picture showing a music
and dance event in front of Buddha Amitayus' pedestal.
The "Reverse Playing" is an important musical playing
technique, whereas Pipa is an ancient Chinese musical

instrument. The dancers have high caps and are naked in
the upper bodies. They wear long waist stripes and long
shawls. Playing Pipa reversely they are dancing very
gracefully. Through skillful brushes the painter manages
to demonstrate the high degree of professional proficiency
of the dancers as well as the superb dancing art during the
Tang Dynasty.

106. 第 25 窟 (榆林窟)　南壁　觀無量壽經變 (全)
Aparimitayur Sutra Episode (general view) /South wall (Yulin Grottoes) / Cave 25

Also called the " Ten Thousand Buddha Valley", the Yulin Grotto is located on the rock walls of the west and east banks of Yulin River (or Tashi River) which is about 70 kilometers to the southwest of the government residence of Anxi County, Gansu Province. There are altogether 42 existing caves built in different times with an accumulated fresco area of 4200 square meters and 259 colored statues, forming one of the largest grottoes bodies among the Mogao Grottoes. The frescoes here are rich in content, good in quality and refined in drawing, winning the prestigious name of "Green Wall Paintings". Picture 106 depicts a painting made in Middle Tang Dynasty based on the "Aparimitayur Sutra" on the south wall of cave 25 in the Yulin Grottoes. This painting is similar to the paintings of early Tang in structure, namely it is composed of three parts, with a large Amitayus Paradise in the middle and horizontal "Future-borns Grief " image and "Sixteen Views" image on the two sides. The paradise in this painting is bit different from the ones found in other paintings in that there are not so many people in it. Rather, the number of figures is made appropriate by taking reference to the exact size of the painting. This treatment makes the painting very clear and eye-catching. Green waters, green meadows, green woods coupled with red pillars and red kasayas in this picture make the Episode decorated more splendidly and brilliantly.

107. 第25窟（榆林窟）
南壁《觀無量壽經變》東側
大勢至菩薩
Mahasthamahratpa Bodhisattva /
South Wall, Eastern Side of the
Aparimitayur Sutra Episode / Cave
25 (Yulin Grottoes)
Created in Middle Tang and
reconstructed later during the
Period of Five Dynasties, Song
Dynasty and Qing Dynasty
respectively, the cave features the
Mahasthamahratpa bodhisattva in
a red skirt and a long shawl,
situated on the eastern side of the
Aparimitayur Sutra Episode.
Holding an instrument in his hand,
he stands barefoot on a lotus seat.
The lines in this picture are simple
and smooth and the colors are light
and yet elegant. The composition
of the figures is mild and refined,
and the dynamic treatment is
natural and gracious.

108. 第 25 窟 (榆林窟)
南壁《觀無量壽經變》西側
觀世音菩薩
Avalokitesvara (Guan Yin) / South Wall, Western Side of the Aparimitayur Sutra Episode / Cave 25 (Yulin Grottoes)

Shown here is the Avalokitesvara statue in a pure white long skirt, situated on the western side of the Aparimitayur Sutra Episode. The Avalokitesvara is standing on a lotus pedestal with his right hand holding a willow twig and his left hand holding a sanitary vase. The painting style, curve drawing, coloring, dyeing and dynamic treatment of the human figures of this picture are all the same as those of Mahasthamahratpa Bodhisattva in the picture of Cave 107.

109. 第 158 窟　　西壁壇上　　卧佛　　　　　Buddha in Parinirvana / Platform, West wall / Cave 158

Built during the Tibetan rule period after 780 AD, this cave is one of the most famous caves depicting parinirvana in Dunhuang Grottos. Depicted in this portrait is a huge Buddha in parinivana in front of the west wall. The whole sculpture is 15.8 meters long, with the head part alone measuring 3 meters. According to the records of Buddhist classics, when the Buddha passes away, he " lies on his right side and becomes profoundly calm on that night." Judging from the overall bearing, the Buddha is lying on his right, with a smile on his face. His expression is natural, relaxed, detached and beautiful. In a true sense, this picture has expressed the nirvana sate that is characterized by a "silent and calm joy".

110. 第158窟　　北壁涅槃變中　　各國王子舉哀　　　　　Parinirvana Episode-Princes in lamentation / North wall / Cave 158

The Grand Parinirvana Scripture records that, when Buddha enters into parinirvana, princes and kings from all countries come to pay a last homage to him. This picture depicts the lively scene of funeral ceremonies attended by princes and kings from all countries. Among them are Zanpu, (King of Tubo), Han emperors, Turks, Ouigours, etc., as well as princes of Afghanistan, Pakistan, Burma, and other South Asian Countries. Since they are from different regions and nationalities, their ways of expressing condolences also vary a lot. Some are depicted as cutting their noses or ears, opening their hearts or abdomens. Others are weeping bitterly or sobbing to express their agony. The tumultuous and crying scenes in the picture form a sharp contrast with the calmness of the Buddha, and reflect the different burial ceremonies of different cultures as well.

111. 第158窟　西壁龕頂　持瓔珞飛天
Apsaras holding gem strings/Niche ceiling, West wall/Cave 158
Holding gem strings with eyes looking downward with ribbons
fluttering in the air, this apsaras is surrounded by color clouds
and is descending slowly from clouds toward the Buddha in
parinirvana as if he is paying homage to the Buddha in parinirvana.
With refined and smooth curve lines, this apsaras isexquisite in
design styles, slender and charming in posture, and elegant in
coloring, ranking among the top artworks of Tang Dynasty.

112. 第158窟　西壁龕頂　吹笛飛大
Fluting Apsaras / Niche ceiling, West wall / Cave 158
Please refer to the caption to picture 111, Apsaras holding gem
strings at thc niche ceiling in this cave.

113. 第 159 窟　　東壁南側　　吐蕃贊普與各國王子

Zanpu, King of Tubo and Princes of various countries / South part, East wall / Cave 159

This picture depicts a scene as a part of Iimalakirti Sutra Episode painted on the southern side of the Eastern Wall
in this cave, in which Zanpu, the King of Tubo are listening to the preaching together with the princes of the
various countries. In the fresco, Zanpu has a tall stature with an imposing air, having a high hat, an underwear with
cross-collar, a commodious gown with turndown collar and long sleeves, and a leather belt with a dagger. He holds
an incense-burner in his right hand and is escorted by two servants leading the way and followed by princes of
various countries who, with their different nationality dresses and adornments, walk slowly. The painter managed
to depict successfully the images of different figures with different identities, postures and backgrounds through a
vivid and concise approach, handling the mutual relationship between people in an appropriate, congruous and to-
the-point fashion. Through the delicate and harmonious layout, the painter reveals that good neighborly relations
among different nations at that time. This outstanding piece of artwork not only reflects the painter's excellent
styles and techniques, but also reflected the high praise the painter accords to the important historical figures.

116. 第159窟　　南壁中央　　觀無量壽經變

Aparimitayur Sutra Episode / Central part, South wall / Cave 159
As one of the best preserved large sized painting in middle Tang Dynasty, this portrait falls into the same category of paintings created in early and Prosperous Period of the Tang Dynasty in terms of theme, design and layout. In the picture, Buddha is preaching, bodhisattvas are listening, orchestras are playing and dancers are dancing face to face. Beautiful buildings, green lotus leaves and red lotus flowers are very vividly depicted by the artist. This picture is strict in design, reasonable in layout, natural in style, strong in strokes and appropriate in figure combination, with elegant and refined coloring.

115. 第15窟（榆林窟）　　前室頂南端　　吹笛飛天

Fluting Apsaras / Southern End, Ceiling of the Front Room/ Cave 15 (Yulin Grottoes)
This cave was reconstructed during the Song Dynasty, West Xia Dynasty, Yuan and Qing Dynasties. However, the Apsaras drawn on the southern end of ceiling of the Front Room is the original artwork of the Middle Tang Dynasty. The Apsaras depicted in the picture is plumpy in face, naked in the upper body, and dressed in a long cloth. With a treasure crown on head and gem strings on the neck, the Apsaras holds the flute on both hands to his lips, playing the flute. His ribbons are flying with the colorful clouds and his shirt swaying with wind, looking elevated in demeanor, elegant in style and charming in appeal. It is also an outstanding representative masterpiece of the Tang Dynasty.

117. 第 159 窟　　西壁南側　普賢變
Samantabhadra Episode / South part, West
wall / Cave 159
Samantabhadra Episode is one of the
Buddhist Episode Pictures in Dunhuang
Grottos as well as a theme picture
corresponding to the Manjusri Episode. In
the picture, Bodhisattvas Samantabhadra
looks very gentle, his right hand on his
knees and his left hand holding a glass
bowl. He sits fully cross-legged on the
back of a white elephant. An escort is
holding the reign of the elephant and the
other carries on his head a plate for
offerings, with a hand. A group of saints
and Bodhisattvas are walking in the sea
of clouds crowding around. Inside the
painting, the beautiful rivers and
mountains complement each other,
forming a charming, magnificent, colorful
and harmonious scene. It indeed deserves
the name as one of the most exquisite
pieces of Dunhuang Artwork.

118. 第 159 窟
西壁龕內南側　　天王 · 菩薩 · 阿難
Lokapala, Bodhisattva and Ananda / South
Side, Niche Interior, West Wall / Cave 159
As the most beautiful groups of colorful
statues erected during the Middle Tang
Dynasty, these statues depict three main
figures: The lokapala has a face painted
with ochre red, upright eyebrows and
widely open eyes, with a tough and fierce
air and a strong and tall figure in his
cuirass. The bodhisattva, 1.39 m tall, with
his body a little bent forward, has an
underwear with flower designs and a silk
skirt of camellias. He is chubby and has
an imposing air. Ananda, 1.30 meters tall,
with a beautiful face, has luxurious
underwear and skirt and also a big kasaya
with trellis pattern. His manner is free and
natural, his air honest and simple. These
statues are exquisite in design and elegant
in coloring, ranking among the
masterpieces of Middle Tang colorful
statues.

119. 第159窟　西壁龕內北側　迦葉·菩薩·天王
Kasyapa, Bodhisattva and Lokapala / North Side, Niche Interior, West Wall / Cave 159
With a height of 1.30 meters, the disciple Kasyapa depicted in the picture has underwear and a long white skirt decorated with beautiful leaf-shaped designs. His right shoulder is bare, with a smile on his face. The bodhisattva, 1.38 m. tall, has a proportionate face with black eyebrows and red lips. He stands graciously on a lotus platform. The lokapala has his arms crossed and his chest thrown out, seeming highly spirited, fierce and courageous. The three statues are different in postures but built collectively a harmonious trio, with two mild, one strong, and one in motion, the other still.

120. 第18窟 (西千佛洞)　西壁　觀無量壽經變
Aparimitayur Sutra Episode / West wall / Cave 18(West 1000-Buddha Grottoes)
Cave 18 of the West 1000-Buddha Grottoes was originally constructed during the Mid-Tang Period and reconstructed in Song Dynasty. This picture depicts the wonderful scenes of the Maitreya Buddha, Western Saints and the Pure Land. This picture is strict in layout, sophisticated in techniques, rich and splendid in coloring, grandiose and magnificent in design. It is a rare treasure best preserved in the West 1000-Buddha Grottoes in the Mid-Tang Dynasty.

121. 第18窟（西千佛洞）　南壁西側
不空羂索觀音

Western Side of South Wall:
Not-empty silk rope Avalokitesvar/
Cave 18 (West Thousand-Buddha
Grottoes)
Not-empty means literally "have the
acquisition necessarily namely". silk
rope, in the Buddhism is musical
instruments used by the Buddha and
Bodhisattvas to restrain the silk
rope asses. Depicted in the picture
is a Notempty Ropebinding
Avalokitesvara painted during the
Tibetan Tubo Period on the western
side of the South Wall of Cave 18 in
the West Thousand-Buddha
Grottoes, one of the Grottoes groups
in Dunhuang. This portrait is beautiful
in face with the Rope-Binding around
the neck., sitting solemnly under the
canopy on the lotus pedestal. The
Bodhisattvas and family depen-dents
surround them. The picture is smooth
in curve lines, elegant in human
posture, rich and refined in coloring,
as a perfect embodiment of the Tang-
style fashions.

122. 第16窟（西千佛洞）　窟頂南披　説法圖（回鶻）

Buddha preaching the doctrine (Uigur) / South of the Cave Ceiling / Cave 16 (West 1000-Buddha Grottoes)

The West 1000-Buddha Grottoes is located in the cliffs on the north bank of the Dang River about 35 kilometers southwest of Dunhuang, Gansu Province, as one of the grottoes groups in Dunhuang. As one of the important constituents of the Dunhuang Grottos Art, it currently has 22 caves in different historical periods, namely 2 in North Wei Dynasty, one in Northern Dynasty, one in North Wei Dynasty, 4 in North Zhou Dynasty, 3 in Sui Dynasty, 3 in Early Dynasty, one in Middle Tang Dynasty, 3 in Late Tang Dynasty, 2 in the Five Dynasties, one in the Huigu Dynasty, and one in Yuan (Mongolian) Dynasty. Cave 16 depicted in this picture was originally constructed in Late Tang Dynasty, and was renovated in Five Dynasties, Song Dynasty, and Uigur Dynasty respectively. Shown in the picture is a group of doctrine-preaching portraits drawn during the Uigur Period, which is well preserved, exquisite in human figures, smooth in curve lines, fresh and elegant in coloring. It is one of the most excellent artworks of the Uigur Period in Dunhuang Grottoes.

123. 第18窟(西千佛洞)　窟頂南披
　　　說法圖與千佛
Buddha preaching the doctrine
and the 1000 Buddha / South of
the Cave Ceiling / Cave 18 (West
1000-Buddha Grottoes)
To draw 1000 Buddha around the
doctrine-preaching portrait is a
commonplace style of layout seen
in Dunhuang Grottoes. Depicted
in the picture is a group of
doctrine-preaching portraits
drawn during the Tibetan Tubo
Period south of the Cave Ceiling
of the West 1000-Buddha
Grottoes. In the picture, the
Buddha is sitting fully cross-
legged on the lotus pedestal under
the Bodhi Canopy, with two
attendant Bodhisattvas kneeling
on both sides of the incense desk.
The 1000 Buddha are sitting on the
lotus pedestal making the "Still
Posture". The portrait has strong
curve lines for strokes, and is plain
and calm in drawing style, unique
in design, and elegant in coloring,
reflecting the aesthetic fashion of
Tang Dynasty.

晚
唐
篇

Late Tang (848-907A.D.)

124. 第14窟　窟頂　藻井
Caisson ceiling / Ceiling / Cave 14
Built in late Tang and reconstructed in Song Dynasty and Qing Dynasty respectively, the cave features a caisson design at the ceiling of the cave which is different from other caisson designs in that, in the central part of the caisson, there are two crossed vajras (pestles) with fangshengs (two intercrossed lozenges, a kinds of devil conquering instrument drawn in the caisson designs with religious connotations) and round flowers as border pattern. On the four sides are depicted images of a group of bodhisattvas coming from four directions to participate the preaching assembly, with identical side ornaments and curtains to the usual caissons. Caissons of this type are rare in the preserved artworks of Dunhuang Grottoes. Its coloring is very mild and elegant, painting refined and orderly, and design concise and to the point. It deserves to be called as one of the masterpieces of Tang Dynasty.

125. 第12窟　北壁　藥師經變　　　　▶
Medicine-Buddha Sutra Episode / North wall / Cave 12
Constructed in the 10th year of Xiantong (869 A.D.) and repaired in the Period of Five Dynasties and Qing Dynasty respectively, this cave has some frescos which were repainted during the Period of Five Dynasties, but this painting is still the original ones in late Tang Dynasty. " Episode of Oriental Paradise of Bhaisajyaguruvaiduryaprabhasa Sutra" is abbreviated as "Medicine Buddha Sutra Episode". Depicted at the center of the painting is the Medicine Buddha holding a medicine bowl and seated upright on the lotus pedestal under the musical tree, preaching " the Moral Will Scriptures Colored Glaze Medicine-Buddha" to the bodhisattvas, disciples, Brahmans, etc. With a balanced and proportionate layout, the picture is well painted with fine and exact techniques. Since there is a caption to the lower part of the picture showing "Oriental Medicine-Buddha Sutra Pure Land Episode", people call this picture as the Medicine-Buddha Sutra Episode.

◀ 126. 第12窟　前室西壁北側　大土
Lokapala / North side, West wall Lobby / Cave 12
This lokapala is also called the Northern lokapala Pi Shamen or Duo Wentian and is one of the four Buddhist Doctrine Protecting lokapalas. The lokapala Vat Sravana is wearing a crown and a cuirass. With a robust body and a majestic looking, he holds a club in his right hand and a pagoda in another. According to Buddhist history, he is a protective god of Buddhism. The Buddhist sutra says that he lived half way up the North Slope of Mount Sumeru, so he is also called "North Lokapala". Exquisitely painted and elegantly colored, this painting is a representative masterpiece of late Tang Dynasty Lokapala Statues.

127. 第12窟　南壁西端　作戰圖
Battle scene / West end, South wall / Cave 12
Drawn on the basis of a story called "Peace and Happiness" in Saddharma Pundarika Sutra Episode, this picture depicts a wonderful scene of an ancient battle between two armies. Battle portrait is the alias name of the Peace and Happiness, in which the armies of two countries are warring with each other on riverbanks. Cavalry of one side launches an assault to pass the river, braving enemy's arrows, and archers of the other side are fully occupied in meeting the attack. In the water, there is a tumult of horses and warriors fallen everywhere. The artist seizes a flash of paroxysm to depict the vivid warring scene with his astonishing ability of synthesis, giving us a deep impression of being placed on the battlefield. The picture is strict in layout, concise in description and condensed in strokes. It is a valuable historical material to research into the Warring History in Tang Dynasty.

129. 第17窟　北壁西側　近事女　▶

Maid-Servant / North wall / Cave 17

Before Tang Dynasty, a woman who received the sila and observed the Buddhist ordination at home was respectfully called "Youpoyi", but after Tang Dynasty, it was called "Maid servant or female attendant". This servant maid is painted on the right side of Hongbian's statue. She is chubby with a round face, wearing a man's robe and holding a long towel in her left hand and a stick in her right one. Gentle, elegant, naive and calm, she is standing under a bodhidruma. This picture is simple and vigorous in curve lines, soft and beautiful in colors, with a rational corporal proportion and a real look. It is a Tang-Dynasty human figure portrait which can rarely be obtained.

128. 第17窟　北壁　高僧像—洪辯

Accomplished Monk Hongbian / North wall / Cave 17

Here you can see the world-famous Scripture Hiding Cave, originally built in the Fifth Year of Dazhong (851 AD), in which more than ten thousand scriptures, articles, documents and thin silk pictures were sealed and preserved. Discovered in 1900 (the 26th Year of Guangxu in Qing Dynasty), the Cave has a door opened on the North Wall of the paved way leading to the 16th Cave, one meter higher than the land level of Cave 16. The statue of the Accomplished Monk Hongbian was originally preserved here, which is 94 centimeters tall, sitting with legs fully crossed and hands placed before the abdomen, making a Buddhist Still Posture. Dressed in through Kasaya, he seems chubby in face appearance with protruding nose and fiery eyes, appearing like a scholarly Accomplished Monk. This picture is refined and forceful in strokes, easy and elegant in curve lines, and vivid and lifelike in human appearance. It is also a rare Tang-dynasty human figure portrait.

153

130. 第17窟　北壁東側　比丘尼
Bhiksu /Eastern Side, North wall / Cave 17
The portrait of attendant Bhiksu shown in the picture is located on the eastern side of Statue of the Accomplished Monk Hongbian on the North Wall of Cave 17. Dressed in Kasaya, he is standing under the Bodhi Tree, holding a flat round fan with the designs of two dragons. On the tree hang the sanitary vase used by the monks, and two birds are flying towards the Bodhi Tree in leafy profusion. This portrait is refined in painting, rich and elegant in coloring. The two chasing birds not only make the whole picture more balanced, but has emphasized the liveliness of the whole picture as well.

131. 第9窟　南壁　擊鼓外道　　▶
Paganish drummers / South wall / Cave 9
Constructed by Zhang Chengfeng during the period of Dashun (890-893) and renovated in Song, Yuan and Qing Dynasties respectively, this fresco depicts a scene of a fighting between Sariputra and Raudraksa painted based on the story of the "Sutra of Sages and Sillies vol. 10." Legend has it that Raudraksa transforms himself into a tree while Sariputra transforms himself into a cyclone blowing down Raudraksa's drum and 6 paganish master-drummers are thus unable to beat the drum. Moreover, the cyclone pulls up the big tree and the long snake loses its fulcrum. Raudraksa keeps on retreat, and sariputra wins the final victory. The six paganish master-drummers have no other choice but to surrender, take the tonsure as a pravrajana (monk) and receive the Buddhist ordination.

第 85 窟　窟頂東披　楞伽經變

Mahayana Lenga-Abadora Sutra Episode / East slope, Ceiling / Cave 85 Constructed by Zhai Farong in Xiantong period (860-874) and renovated in the Period of Five Dynasties, Yuan and Qing Dynasties respectively, this cave features the Mahayana Lenga-Abadora Sutra Episode, drawn based on the Dachenru Mahayana Lenga-Abadora Sutra, depicting mainly the scenes of the Buddha preaching philosophical and theological theories of Buddhism. In the middle is the Buddhist assembly in Lenga where Sakyamuni is invited by King Robana of the big city Lenga to preach there. Preaching scenes of various themes are painted on both ends with texts of explanation. This painting is rich in content, clear-cut in paragraph division, proportionate in structure, orderly in organization, sophisticated in techniques, refined in strokes, and complicated in scheme. It reflects the highly developed painting skills and artistic achievement in late Tang Dynasty.

133. 第18窟　西壁龕内南側　天王像
Lokapala Statue / South Side, Niche
Interior, West Wall / Cave 18
Cave 18 of the Mogao Grottoes was
built in Late tang Dynasty and
reconstructed in Yuan (Mongolian)
Dynasty. Dressed in armature, the
Lokapala Statue shown in the picture
is very fierce in outlook, standing on
the little ghosts with glaring eyes and
a commanding air. This portrait is
mild and elegant in coloring, simple
and vigorous in style, vivid and
lifelike in appearance, clear-cut and
strong in curve lines, sharp-cut in
levels, and orderly but not rigid.
Everything is handled in a perfect
way.

134. 第 85 窟　南壁右上角　鹿母夫人

Madam Deer–Mother / Right upper corner, South wall / Cave 85

Madam Deer–Mother is a scene of a story based on the " Mahaupaya Buddha Sutra". Legend has it that a female deer in Baluna becomes pregnant after eating the excrements of an immortal and later gives birth to a girl in human form but with deer feet. The Deer Girl is brought up by an immortal. Wherever the Deer Girl stands there are lotus flowers. One day, the King of Baluna meets the Deer Girl and is charmed by her beauty. So the king marries the Deer Girl and makes her the first lady with the title of "Madam Deer Mother". After the marriage, a lotus flower is born to her, and King Baluna takes it as an inauspicious sign, throwing it into a pond. One day, the king is playing with his officials on the pond when he notices there is a boy under each of the 500 lotus flower pedals. Later, when these boys become adult, each has the power to defeat 1000 warriors, and the country is safe without any need of arms. Finally, all these 500 princes become Buddhist disciples. On the right side of the picture, outside the palace, King Baluna and his officials are depicted as standing by the pond and a man is picking the flower only to find the 500 princes. Inside the palace, the King and Deer Girl are painted as seated side by side with people saluting them before the palace, meaning that the Deer Girl becomes the first lady once again. The painting is rich in content and the plots of the story are both sinuous, vivid and lifelike. It is one of the most exquisite artworks in late Tang Dynasty Episode Pictures.

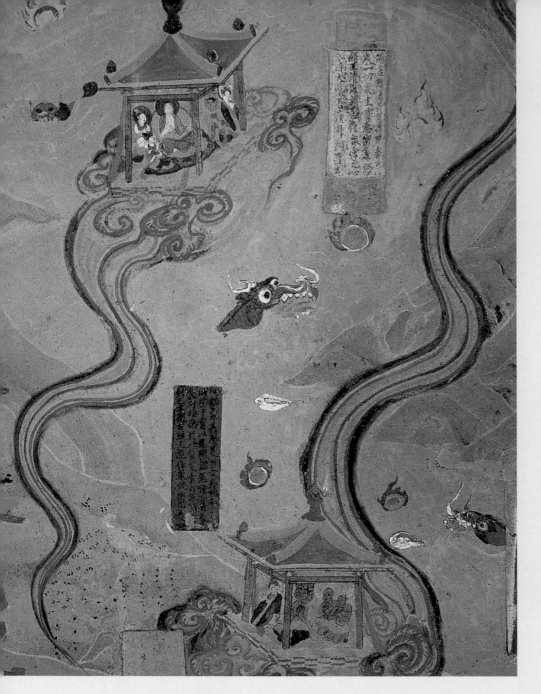

136. 第14窟　北壁　如意輪觀音　▶
Ruyi Wheel Avalokitesvara/ North Wall/ Cave 14

This cave was originally built in Late Tang Dynasty and renovated in Song Dynasty and Qing Dynasty respectively. Ruyi is an S-shaped ornamental object, usually made of jade, formerly a symbol of good luck. As one of the six Avalokitesvaras in Buddhism, the Ruyi Wheel Avalokitesvara portrait shown in the picture is 187 centimeters in height and 188 centimeters in breadth. Wearing Buddhist treasure crown and holding the head with the support of hand, the Avalokitesvara is dressed in luxuriant clothes, looking calm in expression and solemn in posture. With six arms, the Avalokitesvara holds a Ruyi treasure pearl and a Buddhist Wheel in hand, sitting on the lotus pedestal in the divine pond with his legs crossed. This picture is preserved in an intact way, drawn in a refine, delicate and lively manner. It is one of the first-class masterpieces featuring such themes in Late Tang Dynasty.

135. 第85窟　窟頂東披　羅婆那王迎佛

King Robana Welcoming the Buddha's arrival / East slope, Cave Ceiling / Cave 85

This fresco depicts a story plot in the Mahayana Lenga-Abadora Sutra Episode, according to which King Robana, master of the big city Lenga, invites Sakyamuni to preach in the city after Buddha's coming out of the Dragon Palace in the green sea. After hearing the preaching, the king is enlightened and is converted to Buddhism and becomes a Buddhist disciple. This picture is exact in painting, original and freshening in coloring. Despite its relatively small size, it manages to show a scene of broad theme.

1-8

137. 第 85 窟　窟頂　獅子蓮花藻井

Caisson ceiling with lion and lotus images/Ceiling/Cave 85

Caisson ceiling with lion and lotus images is one kind of the caisson patterns in Dunhuang Grottoes. This is the central caisson of those superposed one on another, painted with a lion lying down, some and lotus flowers lines in cloud forms. On the borders are connected spiral squares, lozenges, saint birds, curly herbs and curtains with gem strings as their tassels. On the rims are painted apsaras flying beyond the

Caisson, and on the 4 slopes are Sutra Episodes of Mahayana Lenga-Abadora, Saddharma Pundarika, Maitreya and Buddhavatamsakamahavaipulya. The painting is profuse in content, with the layout well designed to accommodate the various complicated design patterns. With elegant and calming colors, this painting is all sharp-cut in levels, being therefore one of the representative artworks of caisson design in Dunhuang Grottoes.

138. 第85窟　窟頂南披　帷幄夜話
A night chat in a tent / South slope, Ceiling / Cave 85
This painting depicts a story scene of a night chat in a tent painted in the "Saddharma Pundharika Sutra Episode" on the south slope. The painter manages to depict the expressions of the two persons chatting at night, seizing the different bearings of concentration of the two. Besides, it also successfully expresses a feeling of comfort and ease in a vivid way. This picture is concise in layout, mild and elegant in coloring and detached in its artistic style.

139. 第 85 窟　南壁《恶友品》中　善友太子

Friendly Prince in 《Bad friend article》,South Wall. Cave 85.

This picture depicts a moving love story scene that happened between friendly Prince in the ancient Indian state of Benares and the princess of Lishiba State. According to the story, after the friendly Prince obtained a Moni Treasure Pearl, his younger brother friendly seized it away and stabbed the Prince's eyes. The Prince had no other choice but to flee to an alien land (Lishiba State) to keep guard for a garden. Since he often played the Zheng, an ancient musical instrument, in the garden to divert himself from boredom, the Princess of Lishiba State heard of the music and came to the garden to listen. With passing time, the two fell in love and married each other. Later, the Prince recovered his eyesight and led the Princess back to his home country, seizing back the Treasure Pearl afterwards. In this picture, the Prince is depicted as sitting under the green tree playing the Zheng, while the Princess is sitting opposite to him listening attentively. This picture is rich in content, vivid and sinuous in plots, depicting realistically the life scenes of the Prince spending his solitary days in an alien country guarding a closed garden. The whole picture is exquisite in painting style, fresh in coloring, strong and detached in style. It falls into the category of masterpiece pictures preserved from the Late Tang Period.

140. 第 14 窟　　北壁東側　　千手鉢文殊變

1000 Alms-bowl in 1000 Hands Buddha Manjusri Episode /
East of the North wall / Cave No. 14

Shown in this picture is a painting on the east side of the north
wall in Cave 14, painted in the Late Tang Dynasty, portraying a
1000 Alms-bowl in 1000 Hands Buddha. (or Qianshouqianbo
Buddha, page 10 of Depictions on Dunhuang Arts; or
Qianshouqianbo Guanyin, page 62 of Dictionary of Dunhuang
Studies. This book prefers the former name.) In the painting,
the Buddha wears a Buddhist crown, with thousands of alms

bowls in thousands of his hands, sitting peacefully on a huge
lotus pedestal. Beneath the lotus pedestal, the tails of two
dragons are intermingled with each other on the mountainside
of the Xumi Mountain in the sea, with moon and sun rising
high before the body of the dragon. The blue of the sea is in a
harmonious contrast with the red of the lotuses, reaching indeed
the acme of artistic perfection. This painting reproduces the
exceptional painting achievements and the high degree of
professional proficiency during the Tang Dynasty.

141. 第 138 窟　北壁　剃度圖
Scenes of tonsure / North wall / Cave 138
The picture of the Scenes of Tonsure depicts a scene in the
Maitreya Episode. Completed in late Tang dynasty, the painting
shows a scene can be traced back to the same origin as in the
story of Interpretations of the Maitreya Episode in Cave 445
painted in the Prosperous Period of Tang Dynasty. In the painting

a Buddhist Master is cutting the hair of those who wish to become
monks. There are nine other monks with their palms put together
standing piously behind. It is an excellent piece of work in late
Tang Dynasty with vivid portraits and high painting technique,
which is pleasant to mind in content, refined in drawing technique,
mild and elegant in coloring, and smooth in curve lines.

142. 第138窟　東壁北側　報恩經變
Gratitude Sutra Episode / North side, East wall / Cave 138
Constructed in the periods of Guanghua and Tianyou (898-907), and renovated during the Period of Five Dynasties, Yuan and Qing dynasties respectively, this cave features a painting based on a story of Gratitude Sutra. Gratitude Sutra Episode is one kind of Episode Pictures in Dunhuang Grottoes. This picture is identical to Apothecary Episode and Aparimitayur Sutra Episode in that they are all triptich structure pictures, which has developed into a certain kind of fixed painting format by Late Tang Period and during the Period of Five Dynasties and Song Dynasty. In the central part of this fresco is Buddha preaching the doctrine, with bodhisattvas and saints surrounding him. In addition, there are two dancers dancing and waving their ribbons. The palace buildings are grandiose in style and the pictures on both sides are colorful, depicting the happy scenes of the Buddhist fairy land.

143. 第 156 窟　　北壁下部　　宋國夫人出行圖

Procession of Lady of Song / Central Lower part, North wall / Cave 156

This portrait depicts the procession or spring outing of Lady of Henei Prefecture in the state of Song (Madam Zhang Yichao). Painted in the Period of Xiantong (865 AD – 867 AD) in late Tang Dynasty, the original painting is 8.3 meters long and 1.3 meter wide. It is composed of three parts: the first part depicts dancers and acrobats in the procession; the second part depicts carts, carriages and horse-drawn dedans in the procession; the third part depicts the guarding troops

and has an inscription that reads "Lady Song's Procession". The picture shows only the first part of the painting. Please refer to Page 134 of "Chinese Grottoes, Dunhuang Mogao Grottoes" published in 1987 by Antiques Publishing House for information on the other two parts. The painting is well done and gives a glimpse of the grandiose spring procession ceremonies of Tang nobles with a wide scale. It provides a valuable reference to the studies of noble lives in Tang Dynasty.

▼ 144. 第161窟　窟頂西披　觀音＆飛天
Avalokitesvara and apsaras / West slope, Ceiling / Cave 161
Constructed Avalokitesvara in Late Tang period and renovated
in Song Dynasty, this cave features a group of Avalokitesvaras
on the western side of the caisson at the ceiling. The
Avalokitesvara in the picture is elegant and beautiful, and the

skillful musician-dancer Apsaras are gracious in posture,
lively, detached and slender in appearance, with clothing
ornaments flying with the clouds. This portrait is rich in
content, complete in structure, novel in design, smooth
and strong in curve lines, belonging to one of the best
masterpieces in Late Tang Period Dunhuang Grottoes.

145. 第196窟　西壁南側　舍利弗
Saripura / South side, West wall / Cave 196
Constructed by the dharma calya He (Buddhist master)
in the periods of Jingfu and Qianning in Tang Dynasty
(892-893), this cave is also called "Master He's Cave".
Depicted in this picture on the south side of the West Wall
is Sariputra in conquest of Raudraksa. He sits on a lotus
platform under a Bodhi canopy with a calm and composed
air. The Sariputra is capricious in his body form, changing

sometimes into a lion eating an ox, sometimes into a ▶
Lokapala conquering the night ghost. On the upper right
corner are painted a bhiksu (monk) beating a big bell to
inform the victory and 6 beaten paganish masters and their
disciples taking the tonsure to be converted into
Buddhism. This picture is well preserved and vivid,
vigorous in composition, mild and elegant in coloring,
ranking among the exemplar artworks of the Tang
Dynasty.

146. 第196窟　窟頂北披　千佛

Thousand Buddhas / North slope, Ceiling / Cave 196
Many Bodhisattvas' names are now beyond recognition and some inscribed texts are completely fallen off the wall in Mogao Grottoes, but in this cave, names are very clear and also statues are well preserved. 26 well preserved Buddha statues on the north slope of the cave are selected on the South Slope of the Ceiling, who are dressed in red kasayas and seated cross legged preaching under the Bodhi canopy on the lotus pedestal. Some of them are holding alms-bowls in both hands, others are making the preaching posture. There are self-composed in appearance and glowing with radiating vigor.

147. 第196窟　南壁東側下　大勢至菩薩
Mahasthamahratpa Bodhisattva / East
lower part, South wall / Cave 196
Located beneath the Eastern End of the
South Wall of Cave 196, this cave
features a fresco with an inscription
reading "Mahasthamahratpa
Bodhisattva". Wearing a heavenly
costume obliquely over her shoulder,
this bodhisattva has a lotus blossom in
one hand and long ribbon in another.
Painted in profile, she is walking gently
and gracefully on lotus blossoms. The
color of the painting is light but elegant.
The gems on the bodhisattva's hair, her
transparent aura, her pale complexion,
her dignified expression and the waving
skirts and shawls all radiate a sense of
feminine beauty, evidencing the
painter's outstanding painting skills.

148. 第196窟　中心柱佛壇背屏　花鳥紋飾
Flowers and birds pattern / Back screen, Central platform /
Cave 196
Depicted here are the decorative designs on the back screen
of the main statue. It contains pomegranate flowers, curved
herbs, a flying phoenix holding a branch of flowers in its
beak and having a tail in curved herb form. On peripheral
parts are painted Loniceras japonicas in the form of flame
as if multicolored clouds were rolling and flowing quickly
in the sky.

五代篇

Five Dynasties (907-960A.D.)

149. 第 61 窟　　東壁門南　　女供養像

Donatresses / South side, South wall, Gate / Cave 61
Reconstructed during Yuan Dynasty, these cave features
portraits of donatresses from the Cao Family during the
Period of Five Dynasties. This painting merely selects
three representative ladies from the Cao Family. The first
one, with an embroidered Uigur robe is the wife of Cao
Yijin. The caption to her picture is "The son of the Late
Mother of the Northern Uigur State of Shengtian grants
Lady Li, Princess of Qin State…". The second in Uigur
dresses is the daughter of Cao Yijin and the wife of the
Khan. The caption to her picture is "The Princess of Khan

of Ganzhou Whole-heartedly Serves". The third lady
wearing a phoenix crown decorated with pearls and gems
some gold swings, gem earrings, is another daughter of
Cao Yijin. She is also the Queen of Li Shengtian, King of
Yutian. The caption to her picture is "The Kingdom of
Yutian Confers the Title of Nobility on the Empress of
Emperor Zhixiao to Whole-heartedly Serve". As the cave
was created by Cao Yuanzhong, the son of Cao Yijin and
also the son or brother of the ladies in the picture, there
are many inscriptions in the cave showing the titles of
the ladies with addresses such as "mother" and "sister"
etc. in the name of Mr. Cao Yuanzhong.

150. 第61窟　南壁　法華經變

Saddharma Pundarika Sutra Episode / South wall / Cave 61

Saddharma Pundarika Sutra Episode is the abbreviation of Miaofa Saddharma Lotus Pundarika Sutra Episode, belonging to Dunhuang Buddhist Episode Pictures. Painted in Yuan Dynasty, this fresco is the third from the west end. Compared with other frescos in Dunhuang, this fresco has two unique features: one being that it is the one with the riches contents and the other being that its inscriptions are most numerous and also the clearest. In its central part is painted Buddha preaching on Mount Grdhrakta (Mount Vulture). Standing on both sides are Manjusri and Samantabhadra respectively, as well as othe bodhisattvas, 8 celestial dragons, etc. In the central par are seated side-by-side Sakyamuni and Probhtaratna Buddha with Manjusri and Samantabhadra on both sides joining the assembly. In the central lower part are stories of Buddhist sutra and on two extremities, scenes of religious life and lift at leisure time. This painting is well preserved, rich and elegant in coloring concentrated and refined in strokes, clear-cut in level and rich in space dimensions. It is a masterpiece blending many differen painting techniques of ancient times into a complete whole.

151. 第36窟　南壁西側　文殊變
Manjusri Episode /West side, South wall /Cave 36
Being the front room of cave 35, this cave was
constructed in the Period of Five Dynasties and
renovated in Song Dynasty. Manjusri Episode is
one kind of Dunhuang Buddhist Episode Pictures,
and is a thematic picture corresponding to
Samantabhadra Episode. The full name of Manjusri
Bodhisattva is Manjusri. Legend has it that Manjusri
is a 9th generation ancestor of Sakyamuni and all
Buddhas of past time are his disciples. He has thus
the name of "Conscious Father of Three Worlds"
(past, present and future world), and in the
Buddhism, he is the bodhisattva of intelligence. In
this picture are painted all remnants of Manjusri
Episode: Sakredevanam-Indra, Brahma,
bodhisattva relatives and 8 celestial dragons. The
other figures are all destroyed or ruined. This picture
is strict in composition, light and bright in colors,
orderly in organization, and complete in
preservation. Its heavy and beautiful colors radiate
the remaining essence of Tang styles.

152. 第36窟　西壁南側　龍王禮佛圖　　　▶
Dragon-King paying homage to Buddha / South
side, West wall / Cave 36
This picture depicts the scene of the Dragon King
attending the religious gathering to worship the
Buddha together with his family dependents. In
Buddhism, dragon-king is one of devas (god who
protects the doctrine) with a dragon-body and
human-face being, a round face, heavy eyebrows,
and big eyes and wearing crown and waving
ribbons. He is holding a plate of flowers to offer to
Buddha in the deep blue seawater. What is
especially noteworthy is an elegant dragon girl
beside him with chubby face and beautiful eyes, as
if she is holding an incense pot and walking above
the sea surface in a swellfish posture. Red lotuses
are blooming in the blue seawater, and the towering
cliffs are lined with green trees. It is truly a divine
masterpiece blending human figures and scenic
spots.

153. 第61窟　西壁北側　五臺山地圖（局部）

Picture of Mounts Wutai (detail)/North side, West wall/Cave 61

The map of Mounts Wutai is the largest of its kind in existing landscape maps in Dunhuang. It is not only a Buddhist historical remnant picture, but a scenic and figure description picture depicting scenery and humans as well. 13.45 meters long and 3.42 meters wide, this picture has in it the images of several hundreds of monks and laymen and more than 180 constructions. There are titles for each of the temples and peaks depicted in it, namely, Central Platform Peak, South Platform Peak, North Platform Peak, West Platform Peak, Dajianan Temple, Dafahua Temple, Dafoguang Temple, etc. Shown in the picture is the part depicting the grandiose and magnificent temple constructions, with some scenes of mountains, waters and coming-and-going monks. This picture is structured very scientifically and painted very carefully. It is not only grandiose in scene, profuse in layout and orderly in organization, but has also reflected the author's superior Chinese painting techniques and artistic achievements. It has also provided ancient Chinese architecture researcher with a valuable historical referential source.

154. 第220窟　甬道北壁　文殊變　▶

Manjusri Episode / North wall, Tunnel / Cave 220

Depicted in this picture is a new-style Manjusri Episode painting in the third year of Tongguang Period under the reign of Emperor Zhuang of Tang Dynasty (925 AD). It is new in the sense that the Bodhisattva appears in solo instead of in pair with other Bodhisattvas in previous paintings. The second reason why we call it new is because the King of Yutian replaces the Kunlun servant in previous paintings, thus enabling real figures to enter the Buddhist world directly and to make deities coexist with the humans. The Bodhisattva Manjusri in the picture is seated on the back of a blue lion, holding a ruyi (an shaped ornamental object, symbol of good luck). The guide-boy walks before him with joint hand-palms. King of Yutian is holding the bridle of the lion, with an inscription of "The King of Yutian is inspired by the Buddhism and offers his sacrifice..." On either side of this picture is respectively a bodhisattva. The inscription for the one on the west side reads "Avalokitesvara, bodhisattvas of mercy" and the inscription for the one on the east side reads "Portrait of Saint Bodhisattvas Manjusri". On the lower part are painted seven donators of the Zhai Family. This picture is intermingled with red, green and blue colors, with elegant coloring, strong curve lines, smooth and sophisticated techniques and high professional attainment. As a rare masterpiece in the Period of Five Dynasties, this fresco is also the only one with a definite painting date in Dunhuang Grottoes.

155. 第2窟（昌馬石窟）頂部　單飛天
Single Apsaras / Top / Cave 2 (Chanma Grottoes)
Chanma Grottoes are located in the Chanma River about 90 kilometers away from Yumen Town, Gansu Province. There are altogether two places of Grottoes in Chanma, namely, Daba 1000-Budhha Cave and Xiaoyao Grottoes, as one of the Dunhuang Grotto Groups and an important constituent of Dunhuang Grottoes Art. There are 11 existing caves of various ages, but only four caves with frescoes and statues remain. Inside the cave are painted Apsaras, bodhisattvas, flower-bunch designs, etc. Pictures 155,156,161 and 163 are the Apsaras and attendant bodhisattvas painted during the Period of Five Dynasties in the main lobby and ceiling of the second cave of the Chanma Grottoes. Dressed in arm bracelet, hand tachs, divine oblique clothes and a long shirt, the Apsaras is looking ahead, flying in the auspicious clouds and blue sky, His long shirt and dancing ribbons bring colorful clouds with them, piercing the sky. The attendant bodhisattvas look handsome and calm in appearance. Some are holding flowers in their hands; others are putting their hands together to worship piously. This portrait is refined in depiction, exquisite in human figure design, strong and concise in clothes puckers, elegant in coloring and vigorous in style. They are among the few remnant masterpieces in Chanma Grottoes.

156. 第16窟（榆林窟）　　前室北側　吉祥天女　　▶
Auspicious Fairy / North Side of the Front Lobby / Cave 16 (Yulin Grottoes)
Cave 16 of the Anxi Yulin Grottoes was built in the Period of Five Dynasties and was renovated during the period of the Republic of China. This portrait depicts a picture of the Auspicious Fairy on the north side of the front lobby in this cave. The Auspicious Fairy is also called Virtuous Goddess. Dressed in luxuriant clothes and holding an incense pot in hand, she is elegant in posture, looking back into the remote with certain childishness typical of a girl. This picture uses fluent and lively curve lines, mild crimson color and concise layout to add to the feeling of elegancy and beauty in the picture, reflecting at the same time the superb capabilities of the author at drawing.

▼ 157. 第2窟 (昌馬石窟) 頂部 雙飛天
Double Apsaras / Top / Cave 2 (Chanma Grottoes)
Please refer to the caption to "Single Apsaras / Top / Cave 2 (Chanma Grottoes)", Picture 155, top of Cave 2 in Chanma Grottoes.

158. 第98窟 東壁南側 于闐國王供養像
Statue Worshiped by the Emperor of Yutian/ South Side of the East Wall/ Cave 98

This cave was built between 915 –925 AD (see also Page 64 of the Dunhuang Studies Encycopedia) with the fund from Mr. Cao Yijin, and was reconstructed in Qing Dynasty. Depicted in the picture is the Attendant Statue by Li Shengtian, King of Yutian(formerly called Hetian). With a height of 2.82 meters, a high nose and big eyes, tadpole-style moustache, he is wearing a Han-style crown and a dragon robe. His waist is so fat as to hide his knees, with his two feet held by the divine female servants. Holding flowers in his right hand and an incense pot in his left hand, he is worshipping the Buddha in a pious way. The caption reads "God-conferred Zhixiao Emperor of the Grand Dynasty of Yutian is the Cave's Master." The empress is dressed in phoenix crown and big-sleeved jacket, and her necklace is decorated with pearls and jade strings. The caption reads "Lady Cao, Empress of God-conferred Zhixiao Emperor of the Grand Dynasty of Yutian Whole-heartedly Serves." Through relaxed and detached curve lines, deep and elegant coloring and strict layout, the author manages to portray the imperial air of the reverend Emperor to a perfectly vivid degree. ▶

大朝大寶于闐國大聖大明天子

185

159. 第 8 窟（水峽口石窟） 供養菩薩（局部）
Attendant bodhisattvas (partial) / Cave 8
(Shuixiakou Grottoes)
Vulgarly known as Xiadongzi Grottoes,
Shuixiakou Grottoes is located in the lower
reaches of Yulin River 50 kilometers south
of the town area of Anxi County, Gansu
Province. There are 8 existing caves of
various ages, namely, 3 of the Period of Five
Dynasties, 3 in Song Dynasty, 1 in West Xia
Dynasty, and 1 in modern times. Only Cave
8 during the Period of Five Dynasties, Cave
3 and Cave 4 in Song Dynasty are relatively
well-preserved ones. Inside the cave are
painted Manjusri Episode, Western Pure
Land Episode, Six-armed Bodhisattva
Avalokitesvara, Ruyi Wheel Bodhisattva
Avalokitesvara, Doctrine-preaching Picture,
Attendant Bodhisattva, portraits of servers,
1000 Buddha, Apsaras and various flower-
bunch designs, etc. Depicted in pictures 159
and 162 are two attendant Bodhisattvas in
Cave 8 of the Shuixiakou Grottoes. The
Bodhisattvas are exquisite in depiction,
sophisticated in techniques, strong in color
lines, symmetrical in aesthetic designs,
lively and detached in appearance. It is one
of the rarest and best-preserved
masterpieces of the Period of Five Dynasties
in Shuixiakou Grottoes.

160. 第 61 窟　　北壁　　藥師經變　　　Apothecary Episode/ North Wall/ Cave 61
The Apothecary Colored Glaze Light Buddha in this picture is holding a medical pot in his hand,
sitting at the center of the platform with a calm, solemn and mysterious appearance. The sunlight
and moonlight Bodhisattvas are escorting him on both sides, and the various gods and saints surround
them on the rims. Two giant and long dragon-headed poles are located on both sides of the lighthouse.
Before the palace, the would-be children to be reborn are playing in the green pond; the dancers are
dancing graciously in the beautiful rhythm. This picture is preserved quite well, elegant and rich in
coloring, strict and exquisite in layout, grandiose in scale and great in momentum.

161. 第2窟（昌馬石窟）主室
供養菩薩
Attendant Bodhisattvas /Main
Lobby/ Cave 2 (Chanma Grottoes)
Please refer to the caption to "Single
Apsaras / Top / Cave 2 (Chanma
Grottoes)", Picture 155, top of Cave
2 in Chanma Grottoes.

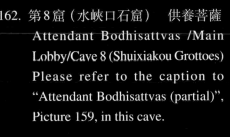

162. 第8窟（水峽口石窟） 供養菩薩
Attendant Bodhisattvas /Main
Lobby/Cave 8 (Shuixiakou Grottoes)
Please refer to the caption to
"Attendant Bodhisattvas (partial)",
Picture 159, in this cave.

163. 第 2 窟（昌馬石窟）主室
供養菩薩
Attendant Bodhisattvas/Main
Lobby/Cave 2 (Chanma Grottoes)
Please refer to the caption to
"Single Apsaras / Top / Cave 2
(Chanma Grottoes)", Picture 155,
top of Cave 2 in Chanma Grottoes.

宋代篇

Sung Dynasty (960-1036A.D.)

165. 第76窟 北壁 十一面觀音 ▶

Eleven-faced Bodhisattva Avalokitesvara/North Wall/Cave 76
Cave 76 in Dunhuang Grottoes was constructed in Tang Dynasty and rebuilt in Song, Yuan and Qing Dynasties respectively. The 11-faced Bodhisattva Avalokitesvara is also called Grand Light Shining Bodhisattva Avalokitesvara, as one of the six Bodhisattva Avalokitesvaras, namely Grand Mercy, Grand Sorrow, Fearless Teacher, Grand Light Shining, Godly Husband, Grand Sanskrit Deep and Far. With eleven faces, this Bodhisattva Avalokitesvara looks kindly in appearance with lotus, treasure pole and treasure cane in hand, making a Fearless Posture and holding the sun and moon in hand. The three Apsaras above him are wearing treasure crowns, long cloth and shirt, flying in the flowing color clouds with the Moni Pearl in hand. Their elegant dancing posture, vivid design, mild and gracious colors, smooth and strong curve lines make any nice word beyond people's capability to praise them. It truly deserves to be called a representative masterpiece in Song Dynasty Dunhuang Grottoes.

164. 第4窟（水峽口石窟） 六臂觀音
Six-armed Bodhisattva Avalokitesvara / Cave 4 (Shuixiakou Grottoes)
Depicted in the picture is a remnant Six-armed Bodhisattva Avalokitesvara in Cave 4 of Shuixiakou Grottoes, pertaining to one of the Bodhisattva Avalokitesvaras featuring Mizong Themes. This Six-armed Bodhisattva Avalokitesvara is wearing a Buddhist Crown with a somewhat leaning head and pretty face, sitting calmly in the round aura. Since this picture is damaged to unrecognizable degree, the attire and hand postures will not be discussed in detail here. This picture is strict, rich and novel in design, exquisite in human figures, elegant in coloring and refined in strokes. It is a extremely rare masterpiece in Shuixiakou Grottoes.

166. 第4窟（水峡口石窟）　文殊菩薩
Manjusri Bodhisattva / Cave 4 (Shuixiakou Grottoes)
Depicted in the picture is a Manjusri Episode painted in Song Dynasty in Shuixiakou Grottoes. The Manjusri Bodhisattva, also called Manjusri Master and Teacher, is renowned for his wisdom and efficaciousness. The Manjusri Bodhisattva in the picture is wearing a three-pearl crown, a shoulder cloth and a jade-stone-decorated necklace with his left hand on his knee and right hand holding a pot. He is sitting calmly on the lotus pedestal on the green lion with legs half crossed. The various Bodhisattvas and saints are surrounded by heavenly dragons and flying long flags, marching in the sea of clouds in a magnificent way.

167. 第17窟（榆林窟）　赴會菩薩
Bodhisattvas Heading towards Gathering /Cave 17 (Yulin Grottoes)
This cave was built in Tang Dynasty, and was reconstructed in the Period of Five Dynasties, Song Dynasty, West Xia Dynasty and Qing Dynasty respectively. The five Bodhisattvas Heading towards Gathering, however, were painted in Song Dynasty. This Bodhisattva is dressed luxuriantly, plumpy in face, fat in body and sedate in appearance. Some are holding flowers, while others are holding their hands together. Some are holding their hands before their chests, while others are holding prayer beads in their hands. Their images are truly vivid and lifelike. Through smooth and strong curve lines, the author shapes clothes ribbons that are mild and flying. The coloring is mild in dealing with heavy colors, exhibiting not only elegancy and beauty, but also the full embodiment of Mr. Wu Daozi's painting skills.

◀

168. 第4窟（昌馬石窟）　供養菩薩
Attendant Bodhisattva /Cave 14 (Chanma Grottoes)
Depicted in the picture is an attendant Bodhisattva in Cave 4 of Chanma Grottoes in one of the Dunhuang Grottoes. Painted in Song Dynasty, this Bodhisattva holds a pot in his right hand and a cloth in his left hand in a gracious way. This picture is well preserved and elegant in coloring, symmetrical in human figure design, smooth and strong in curve lines, ranking among the excellent masterpieces of Chanma Grottoes in Song Dynasty.

169. 第76窟　東壁南側　初轉法輪　▶
Initially Turning Buddhist Wheels / South Side of the Eastern Wall / Cave 76
Originally built in Tang Dynasty and rebuilt in Song, Yuan and Qing Dynasties, this cave features a picture of the Third-Tower Initially Turning Buddhist Wheel of the Eight Spiritual Towers Episodes painted in Song Dynasty. The Eight Spiritual Towers Episodes originated from the Buddhist Scripture of the Names of the Eight Spiritual Towers. Inside the tower are painted three Bodhisattvas sitting cross-legged on the lotus pedestal with joint hands. Outside the tower on both sides are painted three Bodhisattvas respectively with their hands joined, kneeling on the lotus. The captions read "Manjusri Bodhisattva and others are coming to join the gathering" and "Samantabhadra Bodhisattva and others are coming to join the gathering". This picture is rich in content, fresh and elegant in artistic conception, ranking among the most rare masterpieces in Dunhuang Grottoes.

文殊菩薩摩訶薩等來赴法會

普賢菩薩摩訶薩等赴法會

五比丘聞四諦法輪時

第三塔也

諦此震動初轉法輪五人始處揚於四部鹿苑中北界諸述沈迷眾國實今難心愛於玉女愛於智於明解民起之震靜

173. 第1窟（五個廟石窟）　　南壁西側　女供養人
Donatress / Western Side of the South Wall/ Cave 1
(Wugemiao Grottoes)
Chinese Mongolians call Grottoes as Miao or Temple, so Wugemiao means literally Five Temples or Grottoes. Wugemiao Grottoes derive its name from here. Located on the northern cliffs of the Lanwan 20 kilometers west of the county government of Northern Gansu Mongolian Autonomous County, the Wugemiao Grottoes belong to the Dunhuang Grottoes Group, forming an important constituent of the Dunhuang Grottoes art. There are six existing caves of North Zhou Period according to the division of dynasties on pages 225 and 226 of the Dunhuang Grottoes Content List compiled by the Dunhuang Studies Institute, which were renovated in the Period of Five Dynasties, in Song Dynasty and West Xia Period. There are statues inside the caves painted with a number of frescoes, including Devil Conquering Episode, Nirvana Episode, Four-armed Bodhisattva Avalokitesvara Episode, Eight-armed Bodhisattva Avalokitesvara Episode, Eleven-faced 1000-Hand and 1000-eyes Bodhisattva Avalokitesvara Episode, Flashing Light Bodhisattva Episode, Manjusri Episode, Samantabhadra Episode, Apothecary Episode, Vimalakirti Episode, Laboring Ghost Fighting Saint Episode, Water and Moon Bodhisattva Avalokitesvara Episode, Donator's Portrait, etc. Shown in the picture is a donatress on the west side of the South Wall painted in the West Xia Period in Cave one of Wugemiao Grottoes. This donatress is dressed luxuriantly with charming posture, obviously a noble lady in the upper society at the time.

174. 第409窟　　東壁門南　回鶻王供養像　▶
Donator Portrait of Uigur King / South of the Door on the Eastern Wall / Cave 409
Cave 409 was built in Cave 409 in the Period of Five Dynasties and renovated in Uigur and Qing Dynasties. Depicted here is the Donator Portrait of Uigur King, who is plumpy in face, high in nose and small in eyes. Wearing peach-shaped crown and round-collar short-sleeved dragon robe, the King is holding an incense pot in his hand with leather strap around his waist and yak boots on his feet, worshipping the Buddha in a pious way. He is followed by 8 servants, one of whom is holding an umbrella, two are holding a fan, while the others are holding swords and arrows. The plumpy image of the Donator Portrait is the continuation of Tang-style images.

175. 第4窟（五個廟石窟）
東壁《净土變》中　伎樂
Musical Dancers / in Pure Land Episode
on the Eastern Wall/Cave 4 (Wugemiao
Grottoes)
Pure Land Episode is one kind of
Buddhist pictures. Pure Land is called
Utmost Happiness Paradise in Buddhist
scriptures, now generally referred to as
Buddhist World. Shown in the picture
are three musical dancers in the Pure
Land Episode on the north side of the
Eastern Wall of Cave 4 of Wugemiao
Grottoes, painted in West Xia Period.
This musical dancer is naked in his
upper body with short shirt around the
waist and gun in hand. They are dancing

in carnival, blowing copper bungle at the same time. His dancing postures are very wild, elegant and unique, which is rare even in the
numerous remaining Pure Land Episodes Pictures in Dunhuang Grottoes.

◄

176. 第3窟（五個廟石窟）　南壁西側
十一面千手千眼觀音變
Eleven-faced 1000-Hand and 1000-eyes Bodhisattva
Avalokitesvara/ West Side of the South Wall/ Cave 3
(Wugemiao Grottoes)
Built in the North Zhou Dynasty, this cave was
renovated in West Xia Dynasty. Depicted here is an
Eleven-faced 1000-Hand and 1000-eyes Bodhisattva
Avalokitesvara painted in the West Xia Dynasty as
one of the Buddist Mizong themes. This Bodhisattva
Avalokitesvara is wearing Buddhist crown and sitting
among the blooming lotuses, with plumpy and
beautiful face and calm appearance. This picture is
damaged to some degree, but it can still demonstrate
the elegant demeanor of the painting skills of West
Xia Period.

177. 第409窟　東壁北側
回鶻王妃供養像
Donation Portrait of Uigur
Princess / North Side of the
Eastern Wall / Cave 409
The Donation Portrait of
Uigur Princess is located in
the north side of the Eastern
Wall in Cave 409 of Mogao
Grottoes. Dressed in Uigur
costume, she has willow-
shaped brows, small eyes,
even nose and fat forehead.
With long hair covering her
face and earrings on ears,
she holds flower sleeves
before her chests with both
hands, worshipping the
Buddha piously on the
flowers in a calms and
solemn appearance.

178. 第3窟（五個廟石窟） 西壁 天女
Heavenly Fairies / West Wall / Cave 3
(Wugemiao Grottoes)
Depicted in the picture are four Heavenly Fairies in the Laboring Ghost Fighting Saint Episode. The Fairies look pretty in appearance and fine in skin, walking among the color clouds with two hands joined together and two eyes looking ahead. The picture is well preserved and vivid in human depiction, smooth and strong in curve lines, intermingled in mild and deep colors, zigzagged in organization, full but not jammed in layout. It is one of the most excellent masterpieces of West Xia Period Human Portraits.

179. 第16窟　甬道北壁　供養菩薩
Offering Bodhisattvas/North Wall of the Paved Path/Cave 16
Built in Late Tang Dynasty, this cave was renovated in West
Xia and Qing Dynasties. Depicted in the picture are four
Attendant Bodhisattvas painted in West Xia Period on the
North Wall of the Paved Path in Cave 16. Some of these
Bodhisattvas are holding flowers in their hands, some are
holding incense pots, while others are holding flower trays,
walking on lotus. The green covering cloth, the read long
shirts and exquisite crowns and jade strings serve as a foil
to the colorful splendor of the whole picture.

181. 第2窟（榆林窟）　西壁北側　水月觀音
Water- Moon Avalokitesvara / North side, West wall, Yulin Grottoes / Cave 2
Constructed in West Xia Dynasty, this cave was renovated in Yuan(Mongolian) and Qing dynasties respectively. As paintings of this type have water and moon on them, they appear very elegant and graceful and therefore are appreciated by ancient scholars of China. The two Bodhisattva Avalokitesvaras depicted in the West Xia Period in Caves 181 and 183 have a nimbus and are sitting at ease and graciously against a rock, on which there is a vase with a willow branch. A bright moon rises high on clouds. Under the moonlight are long and verdant bamboos, jagged and grotesque rocks and red lotuses floating on the green water. Beside them, a child is painted as coming riding clouds. Radiating an air of peace and harmony, the painting can be best described by a poem written by Tang Poet Bai Juyi, " Upon the calm green ripples, within the vague white light, I witness her, and the void infinite."

180. 第3窟（五個廟石窟）　東壁　維摩詰像
Portrait of Vimalakirti / Eastern Wall / Cave 3 (Wugemiao Grottoes)
The long-bearded old man sitting inside the heavy curtains with fan in hand, bent-forward body and straight-looking eyes is Vimalakirti. He is a reclusive scholar in Pi Ye Li City in ancient India. He is not only proficient at Buddhist Scriptures, but strong at reasoning as well.

182. 第 7 窟（東千佛洞）

東壁上方　飛天

Apsaras / Upper Part of the Eastern Wall/Cave 7(Eastern 1000-Buddha Grottoes)

Located in the banks of the valley 35 kilometers south of the Qiaozi Town, Anxi County, Gansu Province, the Eastern 1000-Buddha Grottoes belong to the Dunhuang Grottoes Group, forming an important constituent of the Dunhuang Grottoes Art. There are 8 existing caves holding frescoes and statues, with three on the eastern rocks and five on the western rocks. There are certain statues and paintings in the caves, including such frescoes as Episode Paintings, Statue Portraits, Mizong Portraits, Donators' Portraits and Decorative Designs. Depicted here in this picture is an Apsaras painted in the West Xia Period on the upper part of the Eastern Wall in Cave 7 in Eastern 1000-Buddha Grottoes. The Apsaras is naked in his upper body, dressed in silk ribbons, baring his left shoulder, baring his feet and decorated by jade strings and arm bracelets. Wearing long trousers and short shirt, he is looking ahead with the right hand raised and left hand spreading flowers. It is indeed of perfect charm and elegancy.

183. 第 2 窟（榆林窟）　西壁南側　水月觀音

Water- Moon Avalokitesvara / South Side of the West wall, / Cave 2 (Yulin Grottoes)

Please refer to the caption to picture 181, the "Water- Moon Avalokitesvara" on the North side of the West wall in this cave.

184. 第2窟（東千佛洞）　唐僧取經

Senior Tang Monk Going on a Pilgrimage for Buddhist Scriptures in India / Cave 2 (Eastern 1000-Buddha Grottoes)
This picture depicts the Senior Tang Monk Xuanzan worshipping Bodhisattva Avalokitesvara across the river together with his disciple Monkey Untonsured Monk, also referring to the same story as in Record of the Journey to the West describing the Senior Tang Monk Xuanzan Going on a Pilgrimage for Buddhist Scriptures in India. However, since the classical novel of the Record of the Journey to the West had not been born by that time, this picture existed several hundred years prior to the story in that novel. It is the one of the oldest remaining story pictures depicting the Senior Tang Monk Xuanzan Going on a Pilgrimage for Buddhist Scriptures in India in Dunhuang Grottoes.

185. 第2窟（東千佛洞）
南壁　菩提樹觀音
Bodhi Tree Bodhisattva Avalokitesvara / South Wall/ Cave 2 (Eastern 1000-Buddha Grottoes)

With one hand raised and one hand holding a sanitary vase upside down, this Bodhisattva is spraying the sweet dews on a hungry ghost with his body somewhat bent, forming an elegant dancing posture. Far away, we can see the blue sky and white clouds. Within short distance, we can see green water and blooming flowers on the Bodhi Tree. It really deserves to be called the place for fairies to live. This picture is elegant and tranquil in artistic conception, unique and strange in human figure patterns, gracious in human posture, bright in ink strokes, and refined in style and organization. It is one of the rare and exquisite Bodhisattva pictures in West Xia Dynasty in Dunhuang Grottoes.

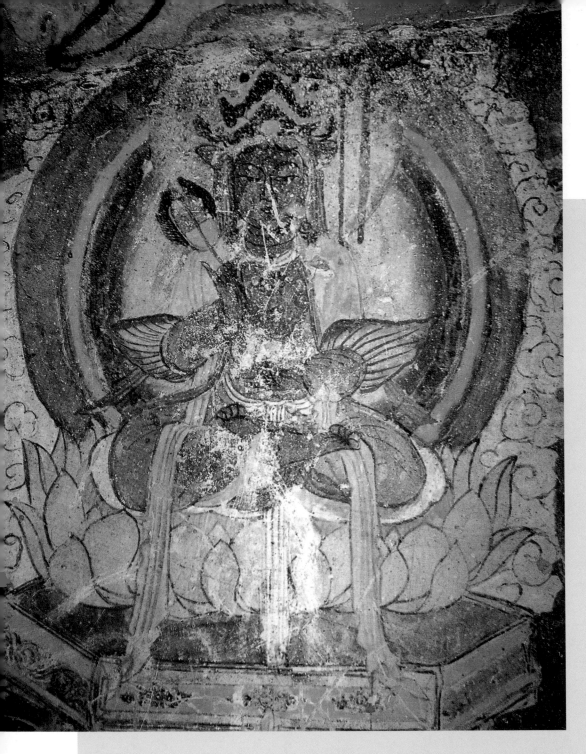

187. 第2窟（東千佛洞）　北壁　水月觀音
Water and Moon Bodhisattva Avalokitesvara / North Wall / Cave 2 (Eastern 1000-Buddha Grottoes)
Water and Moon Bodhisattva Avalokitesvara is a vulgar name for Luojia Mountain Bodhisattva Avalokitesvara. As a renowned Buddhist mountain and sanctum, this mountain is where Bodhisattva Avalokitesvara is supposed to live according to the records of the Buddhist documents. Depicted in the picture is a Water and Moon Bodhisattva Avalokitesvara on the north wall of Cave 2 in Eastern 1000-Buddha Grottoes painted in West Xia Dynasty. This Bodhisattva Avalokitesvara is elegant, divine and pure with beautiful appearance, treasure crown, rising hair bun and lax robes, sitting leisurely on the rocks in meditation. The sanitary vase on the rocks has willow twigs inside. Behind the hill is green bamboo, in the river are blooming lotuses, and across the river the Accomplished Tang Monk Xuanzan is holding his hands together worshipping, while the untonsured monk Monkey King is leading the horse with his hand raised before the eyes to keep watch. The picture is orderly in depiction, elegant and rich in coloring, deserving to be called an excellent masterpiece of Bodhisattva Avalokitesvara portraits in West Xia Dynasty.

186. 第1窟（五個廟石窟）　菩薩
Bodhisattva / Cave 1 (Wugemiao Grottoes)
This Bodhisattva is pretty in facial posture, with the eyes looking ahead, wispy bun and treasure crown on the head, wings on the arms and long hair on the shoulders. Holding a fan in the hand and dressed in divine clothes, he is sitting with full-crossed legs on the lotus pedestal, green cloth dropping down his shoulder. The Bodhisattva looks kindly, leisurely and carefree.

189. 第3窟（榆林窟）　西壁南側　普賢變
Samantabhadra Episode / North side, West wall, Yulin Grottoes/Cave 3
This picture depicts scenes of mountains, uneven woods and beautiful pavilions on hillside and riverbanks, and winding hill tracks surrounding, etc. At the center is Samanta-bhadra Buddha seated in a lotus on the back of an elephant with its feet on lotus flowers. Bodhisattvas, celestial beings and lokapalas walk slowly in a procession on a sea of clouds. Winding roads can be seen in the mountains where some fairy figures are depicted as enjoying the beautiful scenes or resting near the pavilions. This forms indeed a wonderful image and nice scenery. This picture has a delicate composition with various themes and exquisite plastic art, using fine lines to make a beautiful and charming scene. Integrating human figures with natural scenery by employing mild colors and heavy strokes, this picture is covered with a sense of mystery. It is also the crystallization of the hard efforts by the author to draw upon the strengths of multiple sources and various skills to be used for Buddhist paintings.

188. 第3窟（榆林窟）　西壁南側　唐僧取經
Senior Tang Monk Going on a Pilgrimage for Buddhist Scriptures in India / South Side of the West Wall / Cave 3 (Yulin Grottoes)
Please refer to the caption to picture 184, Senior Tang Monk Going on a Pilgrimage for Buddhist Scriptures in India in Cave 2 of the Eastern 1000-Buddha Grottoes.

190. 第3窟（榆林窟）　西壁北側　文殊變
Manjusri Episode / North side, West wall /
Cave 3 (Yulin Grottoes)
What distinguishes this painting from other
Manjusri Episode pictures lies in its splendid
depiction of the grandiose Wutai Mount as
its background. Ranging Mountains, oblique
rainbows, magnificent buildings and mist-
covered water can be seen in the picture.
Manjusri Bodhisattva is seated sedately on
a lotus seat on the back of a lion, walking
on the magnificent scenery with the
accompaniment of other bodhisattvas. This
picture is almost filled with mountains,
rocks, trees, pavilions, buildings and human
figures, leaving only very small room for
other layout items. The layout of the picture
its compact but not disorderly. Through the
author's elaborate arrangement and skillful
roundabouts, towing and aversion, the blank
space below the mountains, the misty fog
and the creeks make the magnificent
mountains demonstrate an air of
spaciousness and unpredictability. The
smooth brushwork, dexterous painting skills,
sophisticated techniques and simple and
elegant colors all fully evidence the painter's
superior painting skills. It also makes the
picture deeper in connotation, serene in
conception and mysterious in appearance.

191. 第2窟（東千佛洞）　南壁　水月觀音 ▶
Water and Moon Bodhisattva Avalokitesvara / South Wallb / Cave 2 (Eastern
1000-Buddha Grottoes)
Please refer to the caption to picture 187,
Water and Moon Bodhisattva Avalokitesvara
on the North Wall of Cave 2 in the Eastern
1000-Buddha Grottoes.

192. 第2窟（東千佛洞）　東壁北側
供養菩薩
Attendant Bodhisattva / North Side of
the Eastern Wall / Cave 2 (Eastern 1000-
Buddha Grottoes)
Depicted in the picture is one Attendant
Bodhisattva of the three 8-armed
Bodhisattva Avalokitesvara Episodes
painted during the West Xia Period on
the North Side of the Eastern Wall in
Cave 2 of the Eastern 1000-Buddha
Grottoes. This Bodhisattva is pretty and
gracious in appearance, sitting on the
lotus pedestal piously with both hands
joined.

193. 第2窟（東千佛洞）　北甬道　藥帥佛
Apothecary Bodhisattva / North Causeway
/ Cave 2 (Eastern 1000-Buddha Grottoes)
Also called Apothecary Glazed Glass
Light Buddha, the Apothecary Bodhisattva
enjoys the reputation as the Medical King
Bodhisattva. Depicted in the picture is the
Apothecary Bodhisattva holding the glass
medical pot in his left hand and a wand in
his right hand on the lotus pedestal,
escorted by two monks with their hands
clasped together. This picture is concise
and exact in layout, exquisite in painting
style, freshening in coloring, strong and
elegant in strokes, ranking among the top
masterpieces of the West Xia Dynasty.

◀ 194. 第5窟（東千佛洞） 緑度母
Green Tara/North Causeway/Cave 5
(Eastern 1000-Buddha Grottoes)
The Green Tara is one of the incarnations of the 21 Reverend Saint
Avalokite'svara, or Tara Bodhisattva
Avalokitesvara. The Green Tara
depicted in the picture is dressed in
green all over with treasure crown on
the head, jade strings on the necklace,
flowers in one hand, and the other
hand on the knees. With his left leg
bent and the right leg drooping, he is
sitting on the lotus warrior pedestal.

195. 第328窟 東壁北側 供養菩薩
Attendant Bodhisattvas / North Side of
East Wall / Cave 328
The two attendant bodhisattvas in the
picture are of a size almost identical to
that of human. They are square and
chubby in faces, and strong in body.
Their silhouettes are clearly marked
with deep red lines, whereas very light
colors are applied to other parts of their
bodies, which gives a relatively flat
decorative impression. Their shawls are
green and their skirts are red. Coupled
with their beautiful crowns and jade
strings, these make this picture bright
in coloring and fresh in layout.

198. 第1窟（五個廟石窟）　南壁
男供養人畫像
Donator's Portrait/ South Wall / Cave 1
(Wugemiao Grottoes)
Donators refer to those who donated
money to construct or renovate the
caves, or the masters of the caves. They
would paint their own images in the
caves they donated. Depicted in the
picture is the portrait of a donator
on the south wall of Cave 1 of the
Wugemiao Grottoes painted in the West
Xia Dynasty. Wearing cloud crown and
round-collar tight-sleeved robe, he is
worshiping piously with both hands
joined, strap around the waist and boots
on the feet.

199. 第2窟（東千佛洞）　東壁北側　▶
三面八臂觀音
3-faced and 8-armed Bodhisattva
Avalokitesvara / North Side, Eastern
Wall / Cave 2
Depicted in the picture is a 3-faced and
8-armed Bodhisattva Avalokitesvara on
the North Side of the Eastern Wall in
Cave 2 of Eastern 1000-Buddha
Grottoes. It belongs to the themes of
Buddhist Mizong topics. This picture
is rich in content, refined in painting,
elegant but not tacky in coloring. It is
a precious Mizong Painting in West Xia
Period.

200. 第2窟（東千佛洞）
　　 北壁　菩提樹觀音
Bodhi Tree Bodhisattva
Avalokitesvara / North
Wall / Cave 2 (Eastern
1000-Buddha Grottoes)
Please refer to the caption
to Picture 185, Bodhi
Tree Bodhisattva
Avalokitesvara, South
Wall, Cave 2 in Eastern
1000-Buddha Grottoes.

元代篇

Yuan Dynasty (1227-1368A.D.)

202. 第 3 窟　北壁　千手千眼觀音　　　　　▶
Thousand Hand and Thousand Eye Avolakitesvara / North Wall / Cave 3

Depicted in the picture is a Thousand Hand and Thousand Eye Avolakitesvara on the north wall of this cave as one of the six avolakitesvaras in Buddhism. The Avolakitesvara has one thousand hands and one thousand eyes, meaning he is very powerful at safeguarding and saving the masses. The avalokitesvara is depicted very handsome, with eleven faces, each wearing a beautiful crown. On each of his hand there is depicted an eye. He stands barefoot solemnly on the lotus platform. On his two sides are symmetrical images of other immortals, such as the Eloquent God, Poshu Fairy, Auspicious Fairy, Fire-headed Warrior Attendant, etc. Above are depicted the images of two apsaras holding flowers offered to the Buddha. Combing the painting styles of North Wei and Sui and Tang dynasties, the painter has successfully depicted the different postures of the figures in the painting, such as the Avolakitesvara's benevolence, the Buddhist Warrior Attendants' fierceness, the Auspicious Fairy's Solemnity, the Poshu Fairy's serenity, the Apsaras' beauty, and so on.

201. 第 4 窟（榆林窟）　南壁東側　白度母

White Tara bodhisattva / Eastern side of the South wall / Cave 4

Originally constructed during the Period of Yuan Dynasty, this cave was restored during the Period of Qing Dynasties. It's a picture of Tara depicted in Yuan Dynasty, which falls into the category of Tibetan Buddhism. There are 21 incarnations of Tara, including Black Tara, Red Tara, and White Tara, etc. AS the Green Tara and White Tara bodhisattvas that are most frequently seen in general, this picture depicts a White Tara bodhisattva. This bodhisattva was wearing a black short skirt, neckband, pearl and jade necklace and arm bracelet and looking straight forward while sitting graciously on the lotus warrior pedestal. Below the lotus pedestal are five bodhisattvas in five lotus flowers with different hand gestures. This picture is preserved perfectly and its shaping, composition, application of dyestuff and coloring distribution and layout are so unique that it surely is a precious document for the study of Tibetan Buddhism.

203. 第61窟　甬道南壁　熾盛光佛
Flamboyant Buddha / South Wall, Tunnel / Cave 61
Depicted in the picture is a Flamboyant Buddha on the
south wall of the tunnel in this cave painted in the Yuan
Dynasty according to the Buddhist classics about the
Buddha. The Buddhist Scriptures say that the Buddha can
radiate bright lights from his pores. That is how the Buddha
is called "flamboyant Buddha". In the picture, the Buddha
is holding a golden wheel and sits very solemnly on the
lotus platform on a large-wheeled cart, surrounded by
miscellaneous immortals such as the gods of 28 stars and

12 zodiac constellations who are wandering in the sea of
clouds. The painting is rich in content, reasonably structured
and carefully plotted, reflecting the artistic attainment of
the author. It is one of the most excellent Yuan Dynasty
masterpieces.

204. 第3窟　南壁　千手千眼觀音　　　　　　　▶
Thousand Hand and Thousand Eye Avolakitesvara / South
Wall / Cave 3
Please refer to the caption to Picture 202, Thousand Hand
and Thousand Eye Avolakitesvara on the North Wall of
this Cave.

234

205. 第465窟　北壁中部　眷屬
Family Dependent / Center,
North Wall / Cave 465
This family dependant is naked
in body, three-eyed, decorated
with jade strings and bracelet
with a high wispy bun. Holding
the Buddhist instruments in the
left hand and articles in his right
hand, his right foot is bent before
his body and his left hand is on
the human figure on the Lotus
Pedestal. This picture is unique
in design, refined and exquisite
in painting style. Although the
color has fallen off a bit, it can
still exhibit its extraordinary
artistic level at the time.

206. 第465窟　窟頂南披　供養菩薩
Attendant Bodhisattva / South
Slope, Ceiling / Cave 465
This Bodhisattva is naked in his
upper body with necklace, arm
bracelet, bangle and ornaments in
his body. Dressed in short shirt,
he holds a lotus and sits with
overlapping knees. The whole
human figure exhibits a strong,
flexible and lively style. The
picture is painted with iron
strings, making the human body
seem more refined and elastic.
The mild blue human body seems
all the more striking against the
rich background color and head
light. The deep red jade strings
and stone-green ribbons add
further to the splendid color of
the picture.

208. 第465窟　南壁中部　雙身曼陀羅 ▶
South Wall Center: Double-body
Mandala / Cave 465

Mandala is the Sanskrit translation with two connotations, one being an altar, the other place to hold Buddhist rites. According to the 20 chapter of the Record of Probe into the Mysterious, Mandala means "the place to hold Buddhist rites", as well as "a round altar". The second chapter of Yanmichao explains Mandala as "the place for saints to gather and all virtues to return". Depicted in this picture is a main statue with double body. The male part is green in color, naked in upper body, six armed, three headed, three eyed, with short shirt around waist. Holding a monk's pot, a warrior attendant, a sword, a wheel, a lotus in hand, it carries the female part in his arms. The female part is in blue, naked in body, three eyed, with high wispy bun in hair. Holding a wheel, a lotus, a warrior attendant, a sword in hand, it also carried the male part in her arms. This picture is vivid in depicting human expression, unique in design and implicative in connotation.

207. 第465窟　東壁門南　護法
Doctrine Protector / South of the Door on Eastern Wall / Cave 465
Depicted in the picture is the God of Doctrine Protection painted in the Doctrine Protector Mandala south of the door on the Eastern Wall in Cave 465 of Mogao Grottoes. This god of Doctrine Protection is red in hair, three-eyed and naked in upper body, with two arms bent before the chest. Holding Buddhist instruments in his hand, he makes a crouching posture with two legs forked. The human figure in this painting is weird in design, vivid in appearance, refined and strong in strokes. It is a masterpiece in Yuan Dynasty portraits.

209. 第95窟　南壁西側　長眉羅漢
Long-browed Arhat / West Side, South Wall/
Cave 95
Also known as Pindolabharadvaja£¨the
Long-browed Arhat is the eldest of six
arhats. This picture was painted according
to a Buddhist scripture translated by
Senior Monk Xuanzan in Tang Dynasty.
The appearances of the arhats vary from
one to another. The arhat in picture is
kindly in appearance, dressed in Kasaya,
with long eyebrows dropping below his
knees, high-rising nose and forehead, and
both arms in a cane. Before him, a disciple
is supporting and escorting him to sit on a
backrest-shaped armchair. This portrait is
true to life, unsophisticated and harmonious, exhibiting the amicable true love
between the master and the disciple.

210. 第465窟　南壁東側　大幻金剛　▶
Dahuang Warrior Attendant / Eastern Side,
South Wall / Cave 465
Dahuang Warrior Attendant is one of the double-
body statues the Buddha is incarnated into so
as to subdue the desirous masses. In blue overall,
he has three faces and 16 arms. Depicted in the
picture is the double-body statue on the eastern
side of the south wall, with the two main statues
naked all over. The male statue is in blue,
holding the female statue in arms with the left
hand holding a bow and the right hand putting
the arrow in place. The female statue is in red
and brown, holding the male statue in arms with
both hands putting arrow and bow in place. This
picture is strict in design, precise in layout, vivid
in image depiction, strong and detached in
strokes. It is indeed a masterpiece from a master-
hand.

211. 第6窟（東千佛洞）　北壁　文殊變
Manjusri Episode / North Wall / Cave 6
(Eastern 1000-Buddha Grottoes)
Manjusri is full named as Manjusri Master as one of the various
Bodhisattva portraits, appearing often together with the
Bodhisattvas Samantabhadra. But this picture is an exception.
Instead of adopting the commonplace approach of letting Manjusri
appear side by side with Bodhisattvas Samantabhadra, the author

merely used the Bodhisattva Manjusri as the main body
against the background of overlapping mountains and
smoggy scenery in remote hills. This Bodhisattva is squared
and round in face, dressed in shoulder cloth, holding a ruyi
in hand, solemn in expression, and sitting on the lotus
pedestal on the back of the lion with fully crossed legs, a
three-pearl crown on head.

212. 第465窟　北壁　歡喜金剛

Happiness Warrior Attendant / North Wall/
Cave 465

Drawn according to the Tibetan Buddhist
Mizong themes, the contents of the frescoes
in this cave are indeed rare to find in
Dunhuang Grottoes. In Tibetan Buddhism,
the Buddha falls into the category of being
Buddhist body in nature, also named
therefore as "Buddhist body by nature".
The reason why a Bodhisattva shows his
real body is to release the souls of people
from purgatory, therefore called "Doctrine
Regulating Buddhist Body". And the Bright
King takes on the angry form upon the
command from the Buddha to destroy all
enemies and devils, therefore called
"Commanding Buddhist Body". Depicted
in the picture is a double-body Buddha at
the center of the North Wall, also named
Happiness Warrior Attendant. In blue all
over, the Warrior Attendant is tall and
strong, with skeleton pearl string around
neck, three eyes and three head on both
sides and three eyes. Holding the pot in
hand, it is holding the female part in arms.
The female part is in deep red with one face,
two arms, and three eyes. Naked in body,
it is holding the moon-shaped falchion with
the right hand, holding the warrior attendant
in arms at the same time. This picture is
sharp in strokes, at will in curve lines, free
minded in style, implicative in connotation.
With the unique artistic style of the Sakya
School, this picture is a rare-to-find Tibetan
Buddhist Mizong Thematic masterpiece.

213. 第 2 窟 (東千佛洞)　東壁南側
供養菩薩
Attendant Bodhisattva / South Side,
Eastern Wall / Cave 2 (Eastern 1000-
Buddha Grottoes)
Depicted in the picture is an attendant
Bodhisattva painted in the West Xia
Dynasty, according to the division of
dynasties in the General Table of
Contents in Dunhuang Grottoes. The
appearance and sitting posture of this
Bodhisattva are similar to the
attendant Bodhisattva painted in Yuan
Dynasty on the south slope of Cave
465 in Mogao Grottoes. This picture
is well preserved, refined in painting,
deep in coloring, slender and pretty
in image, being therefore filled with
anima. It is one of the few Mizong
Thematic pictures preserved in
Dunhuang Grottoes.

絹畫篇

Silk Paintings

◄ 216. 舍利弗
Sariputra
This is a precious Tang Dynasty silk painting, being the only one of its kind left in Dunhuang Grottoes. Painted in Tang Dynasty around 800-900AD, this painting is 95.9 centimeters tall and 51.8 centimeters wide. Depicted in the picture is the Sariputra standing on the side of Buddha Sakyamuni preaching the doctrine in green Kasaya, with one hand pushing the sleeves and the other holding the incense pot.

217. 報恩經變 ►
Gratitude Sutra Episode
Painted in Tang Dynasty in the first half of the 9th century, this painting, 160.8 centimeters tall and 121.6 centimeters wide, is one of the best preserved masterpieces of it kind in the Scripture Hiding Cave in Dunhuang Grottoes. In the middle of the picture is depicted episode of Gratitude Sutra; on the left side is a story about how a man cuts his own flesh to feed his parents; and in the upper left corner is the story of the Deer Girl; in the lower part is the story of good friends and bad friends of the Prince. At the center of the painting is the Buddhist paradise full of brightness and happiness. Above there is the magnificent Buddhist temples, etc. The painting is exquisite in depiction, square in organization and bright in color. Although the color has faded away due to long years of evolution, it still exhibits a splendid color.

218. 水星
圖爲《熾盛光佛》圖中的五星神之一
水星（即辰星）。
Mercury
Depicted in the picture is the goddess of Mercury as one of the five Planet Gods in the Portrait of Flamboyant Buddha. In the painting the goddess of Mercury is depicted as wearing a monkey shaped crown and wearing a female costume. She has a writing brush in one hand and paper in another hand.

219. 熾盛光佛　　　　　　　　▶
Flamboyant Buddha
Painted in the fourth year of Qianning Period, Tang Dynasty (897 AD), this silk painting is 80.4 centimeters tall and 55.4 centimeters wide. Based on a Buddhist Sutra, its contents are quite similar to the fresco on the south wall of Cave 61 built in Yuan Dynasty. In this painting, the Buddha is depicted as wearing a red kasaya with bright radiation. He sits solemnly on the lotus seat in a double-wheeled ox-driven cart, with banners on its rear. Gods of five planets are escorting him respectfully on both sides of the cart as well as behind it. The atmosphere is both solemn and mysterious.

220. 金 星
圖爲《熾盛光佛》圖中的五星神
之一金星(即太白星)。
Venus
Depicted in the picture is the
goddess of Venus as one of the five
Planet Gods in the Portrait of
Flamboyant Buddha. Painted as
wearing a bird shaped crown and
white female costume, she is
holding a Pipa in her hand.

221. 土 星　　　　　　　　▶
圖爲《熾盛光佛》圖中的五星神
之一土星(即鎮星)。
Saturn
Depicted in the picture is the
goddess of Saturn as one of the five
Planet Gods in the Portrait of
Flamboyant Buddha. The deity of
Saturn is depicted as wearing an ox
shaped crown. He is holding a zinc
cane in his hand, being naked in
upper body and bare in both feet.

222. 九龍灌頂

New-born Prince Abhisek (Buddhist Baptism)

Depicted in the picture is the scene of nine dragons bathing the Prince by pouring lukewarm water from their mouths. In the center, the chubby Prince Siddhartha is standing in a basin in lotus form with maids of honor busy with serving him. The painting is unsophisticated in structure, deep in strokes and condensed in style.

223. 離 別 ▶

Farewell

This painting depicts the moving scene of farewell by Prince Siddhartha, who decides to leave the family to observe the Buddhism. At midnight in one day, he escaped the city on horseback and enters deep mountains, where he parted his wagoner and the white horse. In this picture, the Princess is seated on the rock, the wagoner is crying with his face hidden in hands, and the white horse is kneeling to bid farewell to the Prince. The scenery is moving and sorrowful, but is also reflects the hot and harmonious love between the Prince, the wagoner and the white horse.

224. 鹿 女　　Deer Girl

The painting depicts the scene of the story about lotuses growing under the feet of the Deer Girl. The story goes like this: there are two immortals living in south cave and north cave respectively. The immortal in the south cave pissed in a spring. A female deer drunk the water accidentally and unexpectedly gave birth to a girl with human form but deer feet. One day, the Deer Girl distinguished her fire accidentally. When she went to the north cave to borrow the light, there grew a lotus flower in each of her footsteps. Shown in this painting is exactly the scene of lotuses growing under her feet with every step.

225. 童子　　Children
　　Depicted in the picture are three naïve and innocent children playing in a sea of lotus flowers. Well painted with bright colors, concise layout and strong curve lines, it is a typical painting showing the fashions in Tang Dynasty.

234. 日藏菩薩

Sun Bodhisattva

Shown here is the Sun Bodhisattva and Moon Storage Bodhisattva on the eastern and western sides of picture 231, the Thousand Hand and Thousand Eye Avolakitesvara. The two Bodhisattvas are holding sacrifices on their hands, paying their tributes piously by kneeling on the lotus pedestal. This painting is exquisite in painting, bright in coloring, and complementary in terms of layout and connotation.

235. 觀音菩薩 ▶

Bodhisattva Avalokitesvara

With a height of 77 centimeters and a breadth of 48.9 centimeters, this portrait was painted in the tenth year of Tianfu in Tang Dynasty (910 AD) and is now kept in British Museum. This Bodhisattva Avalokitesvara is chubby in face, solemn and tranquil in expression. Wearing a Buddhist crown, he is holding a sanitary vase with his right hand and raising a willow twig with his left hand. With a jade string around his neck, he is sitting on the lotus pedestal with bare feet. On the eastern and western sides of the Bodhisattva Avalokitesvara is painted a monk holding an incense burner in hand as well as a donator holding the sacrifices in hand, serving beside him piously. Above the western side is a poem, while above the eastern side is a caption reading "Mr. Zhang Youcheng Wholeheartedly Serves…". Although this picture was painted in the Period of Five Dynasties, it is nonetheless no worse than the artistic charm of Tang Dynasty paintings in terms of painting techniques such as layout, human figure and coloring.

237. 觀世音菩薩　▶
Bodhisattva Avalokitesvara
Measuring 74.7 centimeters vertically and 55.5 centimeters horizontally, this portrait of Bodhisattva Avalokitesvara was painted in Late Tang Dynasty, or the second half of the 9th century. It is one of the numerous silk paintings preserved in the Scripture Hiding Cave in Dunhuang Mogao Grottoes. The Bodhisattva Avalokitesvara in the painting is wearing a Buddhist crown, with a chubby face, composed expression, pretty and solemn appearance. With small eyebrows and long eyes, his eyes are looking ahead. Dressed in oblique heavenly clothes, he bares his chest and arms. Holding a sanitary vase with his right hand and a long cloth with his left hand, he is standing on the lotus with the long cloth flying vigorously in the air. Two attendant children are dressed in earthly costumes with flowers in hand and two hands joined, serving on both side of Bodhisattva Avalokitesvara. This picture is novel in design, exquisite in description, smooth in curve lines, detached and elegant in connotation, gracious and sublime in style. It is a rare artistic masterpiece in Tang Dynasty.

236. 月藏菩薩
Moon Storage Bodhisattva
Please refer to the caption to Picture 234, Sun Bodhisattva

238. 地藏菩薩

Ksitigarbha Bodhisattva
This is located in the left bottom of Picture 227, the Thousand Hand and Thousand Eye Avolakitesvara. Around him is filled with greenery, and above him are blooming flowers. Dressed in a Kasaya, the Bodhisattva is sitting fully cross-legged on a bright lotus pedestal, holding a flaming pearl in his right hand, and a zinc cane with his left hand. At the right bottom of the picture is the Daoming Monk, serving beside the Bodhisattva with both hands joined together. Captions can be found at the right top of the picture, reading "it is about time for Daoming Monk to return". At the left bottom, a lion is under the left foot of the Bodhisattva, and caption can be found at the left top part saying " Time for the Ksitigarbha Bodhisattva to come here for an inspection". The picture is preserved well, compact in layout, sophisti-cated in the dyeing technique, and fresh as new in terms of coloring. It is a top masterpiece in the silk paintings of Nor-thern Song Dynasty in Dun-huang Grottoes.

圖版說明

Plate Specifications

圖版説明

北涼篇（公元 421 — 439 年）

1. 第272窟　西壁南側　供養菩薩
該窟始建于十六國時期，在五代期間重修。圖中的供養菩薩上下四排，共二十身，位於西壁南側。此組菩薩裸上身，披帛巾著天衣。有的席地而坐，有的蹲踞，手勢臂姿各异，真是嬌健裊娜，神情恬淡，是敦煌石窟遺存的早期壁畫之一。

2. 第272窟　西壁龕内北側　脅侍菩薩
圖爲該窟西壁龕内主尊北側的一身脅侍菩薩；此菩薩面型橢圓，手指纖細，飄帶對稱飛舞，頭戴蔓冠，描繪細致入微，綫條勁挺有力，動態處理自然大方。

3. 第275窟　西壁　交脚彌勒菩薩
這個窟始建于十六國時期，后在宋代重修。圖中的交脚彌勒菩薩是莫高窟現存早期塑像中最大的一尊彌勒菩薩像，高3.4米，右手殘、左手撫膝作"與願印"，揚掌，交脚，坐雙獅座，頭戴三珠寶冠，項圈飾鈴，胸飾瓔珞，腰束羊腸裙，裙上折貼泥條并加陰刻綫紋。此菩薩神情莊静，飄逸磊落，高雅超凡，是莫高窟早期塑像的杰出代表作之一。

4. 第272窟　窟頂　疊澀式藻井
該藻井飾蓮花、火焰和飛天，桁條飾忍冬圖案，四周爲天宮伎樂。宮殿欄墻以下繪的是飛天和千佛，窟頂正中是浮雕，中心繪一朵盛開的蓮花，角飾火焰紋和半裸體飛天，外周飾忍冬紋。從下向頂望去，看到那高遠的穹窿巨頂是那麼的邈邈無際，但又是那麼的真真切切，仿佛古代藝術大師們造窟、繪畫的情景就在眼前。

5. 第272窟　藻井外沿　伎樂與飛天
飛天又稱之香音神，是佛國世界歌舞、散花之神。此圖是圍繞藻井四周的部分飛天和伎樂，它結構完整統一，人物姿態各有神彩，但絶不雷同；特別是那飛天的飄逸，伎樂體態的優美，粗獷豪放暈染的粗綫條，能讓你如醉如痴。

6. 第275窟　南壁　飛天與供養菩薩
此窟建造于十六國時期，在宋代時期重新修復。圖中的飛天與供養菩薩是位於本窟南壁的一組，該飛天構圖精美，菩薩造型生動，姿態婀娜。

7. 第268窟　西壁龕内　交脚佛像
此窟始建于十六國時期，在隋和宋代重修。交脚佛，一般通稱爲"彌勒佛"。本窟龕内的交脚佛是十六國時期原作，但佛像的頭部却是宋時期補塑的。此佛像高0.76米，右袒袈裟，交脚坐於龕内。龕外兩側繪有供養菩薩和飛天；龕楣飾火焰紋，兩端繪的是莫高窟唯一的希臘式柱頭。

8. 第275窟　北壁中層　毗楞竭梨王本生
毗楞竭梨王是釋迦牟尼前生，也是敦煌石窟早期的"本生"故事畫之一。圖中繪的是毗楞竭梨王爲求法心切，甘願讓勞度叉在自己身上釘釘的動人場面。畫面上勞度叉左手執釘，右手揮錘向毗楞竭梨王胸部釘釘，而該王却神態安然。這充分表現了毗楞竭梨王求法的虔誠之態。

9. 第275窟　北壁中層　月光王本生
該圖是依據《賢愚經·月光王施頭緣品》繪制而成的，亦屬敦煌石窟早期的"本生"故事畫之一。故事説：月光王賢達心慈、常做善事，受到民衆的擁戴。一小國國王毗摩斯很忌妒，就用重金收買婆羅門勞度叉索取月光王人頭；於是勞度叉就到月光王處乞頭，月光王慷慨允諾，并和衆人説，我曾以頭施人九百九十九次，再施一次既滿千數，就讓我實現施頭千次的心願吧，於是衆人就遂勞度叉砍月光王頭而去。圖爲月光王施頭情景，有一侍者胡跪于月光王身前雙手捧盤盛三頭，以示曾已施頭千次。

北魏篇（公元 439 — 535 年）

10. 第254窟　南壁東端　薩埵那太子本生
這個窟在隋代時期重修。圖爲薩埵那太子舍身飼虎的故事場面。故事説：薩埵那太子和兩兄長出外游獵，見山中一只母虎，因饑餓將要吞食幼虎。爲救母虎和數只幼虎，薩埵那以干竹刺頸出血，舍身投崖喂虎，兩兄馳返宮中告訴父母。國王和夫人急忙趕至山谷，抱尸痛哭，收遺骸起塔供養。此畫面故事情節生動感人，構思獨特，布局緊密，是早期故事畫中的杰出作品。

11. 第259窟　北壁龕内　禪定佛像
此窟在宋代時期重修。禪定佛像，即是修禪入定的坐佛形象。圖中的禪定佛，高0.92米，身穿通肩袈裟，結跏趺坐，兩手相叠施禪定印，椎髻，神態莊静，作沉思狀。造型嚴謹，古樸大方；設色沉穩濃艷，是敦煌石窟塑像的代表作品之一。

12. 第254窟　南壁東端　薩埵那太子本生（局部）

請參見圖10《薩埵那太子本生》文。

13. 第254窟　北壁前部中層　難陀出家

此圖是描繪難陀出家的一個精彩故事場面。故事說：釋迦牟尼強迫異母弟弟難陀剃度出家，但其弟經常思念自己美貌的妻子。一日偷跑回家，被釋迦發現，將他嚴加訓戒，并領他游遍天宮，觀諸天女；復游地獄，見湯鑊之刑。觀后難陀悔悟，一心從佛出家，后成爲羅漢。圖中佛像右下的比丘即是難陀；東、西下角是描繪難陀與妻子依戀之情的圖景。該畫內容豐富、生動、真實，構思精密，布局緊湊，是敦煌石窟中僅有的一幅精品。

14. 第257窟　窟頂　平棋圖案

該窟在宋代重修。平棋圖案："平棋"俗稱之爲房頂的天花板，"圖案"即是爲建築物裝飾所繪的各種圖形。本圖位於第257窟后部窟頂東南角上的一方平棋圖案；該圖案用各種紋樣爲邊飾，外層四角繪飛天，中層四角繪山形火焰紋，中心繪四天人在蓮池中裸泳。此畫構圖方式獨特，圖案描繪自然，古樸有趣，但綫條生澀不暢、粗細不一，形態古拙而簡勁，這就鮮明地體現了中國早期繪畫的特征。

15. 第257窟　中心柱上層南向龕　思維菩薩

這是位於中心柱上層，南向龕內的一身半跏彌勒菩薩，一般通稱思維菩薩（屬禪定造像），高0.92米。該菩薩右脚叠于左膝上，右手一指支頤，上身向前微附卜視，作思維之狀，展示了坐禪入定時的澄心静慮、萬念皆空的境界。

16. 第257窟　西壁南端《九色鹿本生》中　溺人獲救

17. 第257窟　西壁南端《九色鹿本生》中　鹿與國王

圖16、17是依據《佛說九色鹿經》繪制而成的。描繪九色鹿干從水中救起一落水人，落水人拜謝鹿王，鹿王與國王對話的一段故事情景。故事說：鹿王從恒河中救起一名落水人，落水人爲了感救命之恩向鹿王發誓，決不露其行踪。王后夜夢九色鹿，欲得其皮作褥，得其角爲飾；於是國王重賞捕鹿。落水人見利忘義，領著國王前去捕殺九色鹿。九色鹿面對國王述說原委，國王聽后深受感動并立即下令禁止捕鹿。后落水人和王后均得報應而死。畫面爲橫卷式，總長度爲385厘米，總寬度爲96厘米；根據內容需要，故事情節從西端向

中間發展，形成高潮而結束。此畫結構完整，構圖新穎，生動，綫條流利順暢，色彩瑰麗和諧，是敦煌石窟北魏時期故事畫中的上品。

18. 第251窟　北壁《説法圖》中　雙飛天

此窟在五代和清代重修。圖中兩飛天屬莫高窟的早期飛天，上身裸體，披長巾，穿長裙，在空中漫游、飛翔，其飄帶隨風而起，翩翩起舞。

19. 第257窟　北壁前部　飛天

這是位於257窟北壁前部的一組飛天。此飛天綫條粗獷、流暢有力；飛翔姿式各异，姿態優美無比。這充分表現了北魏時期繪畫藝術的獨特風格，和古代畫師們的驚人創造才能。

20. 第263窟　南壁　降魔變

此窟在五代、西夏時期重修。圖爲釋迦佛與魔王波旬及衆魔鬥法的故事場面。該圖正中繪的是釋迦佛結跏趺坐，一手執衣裾，一手作'指地印'，形體高大，泰然自若。佛的兩邊繪的是形狀怪异、狰獰凶惡的衆魔。這幅畫構圖嚴謹，主題突出；衆魔的騷擾、動亂與釋迦佛鎮定自若形成了鮮明的對比。

西魏篇（公元535—556年）

21. 第249窟　窟頂南披　帝釋天妃

該窟在清代時期重修，但本圖乃是西魏時期原作。帝釋天妃也稱西王母，據《山海經》記載，西王母居住在西海之南，流沙之濱，赤水之后，黑水之前的昆侖山上；其形是"戴勝虎齒，有豹尾"，顯然是原始社會的圖騰形象。而此圖繪的却是貴夫人形像，乘三鳳駕車，身穿大袖襦拱手而立，前有持節揚幡和乘鸞仙人、烏獲、飛天及方士騎鳳相隨，后有文鰩，白虎，開明尾隨，在彩雲中列隊西行。下部繪的是黃羊、野牛在森林中歡快奔跑的情景。

22. 第432窟　中心柱東向龕　彩塑一鋪

這個窟在西夏時期重修。圖中的彩塑爲西魏和北周期間塑造。該佛像屬善跏坐佛，手施"説法印"，外穿袈裟，內著僧衣，束小結，佛光飾火焰紋。龕楣飾忍冬化生圖案，龕楣上方飾影塑供養菩薩，龕外兩側塑脅侍菩薩立像。此鋪彩塑色彩豐富、絢綺明麗，人物組合疏密得當，裝飾圖案繪制精美，體現了當時塑造人物與裝飾繪畫已達到了極爲精湛的技藝高度。特別一

提的是龕外左右兩身脅侍菩薩，被作者塑造的含姿蘊彩，寧靜妙麗，不愧被稱之爲敦煌石窟塑像的代表作。

23. 第249窟　窟頂西披　阿修羅
阿修羅，譯爲"非天"，是古印度神話中的惡神。據佛經記載：他前世貧窮，經常渡河砍柴，有一次落水，幾乎被淹死。一天，關支佛化一和尚到他處乞食，吃完后將食鉢擲到空中飛旋而去，於是窮人發願，盼來世身形長大，渡深水不過膝。由於他對關支佛施舍過飯食，果然長大了身軀，身高超過了須彌山，立於海中不過膝。圖中阿修羅，赤身四目、四臂，形體高大，腳立于大海之中，手擎日月，雙龍護衛。身后繪的是須彌山，山左側繪的風神，烏獲，右爲雷公，電母；圖下方繪的是漢式建築，上方繪的是西域樣式的宮殿。

24. 第249窟　窟頂北披東下　野猪群
圖爲一頭母猪帶領六頭仔猪在林中奔走覓食的情景。此畫綫條簡潔流暢，動物描繪生動活潑，栩栩如生。

25. 第249窟　窟頂北披下部　狩獵圖
這是一幅描繪古代游牧生活的真實圖景；圖中遠山叢林有二獵人在騎馬奔馳追捕獵物，其中一獵人正回身拉箭射虎，一獵人正舉槍捕捉驚慌奔跑的黃羊。此畫山樹參差錯落；動物多姿，人物組合疏密得當，布局合理，情景交融；特別是黃羊的驚慌奔跑、虎的凶猛及獵人騎馬狂奔狩獵的動態，被作者捕捉的恰如其分，表現的淋灕盡致。

26. 第285窟　窟頂東披
此窟在中唐、宋代、西夏和元代時期重修。窟頂東披中間繪的是二力士舉摩尼寶珠和開放的蓮花，兩側繪的是中國古代神話傳說中的伏羲、女媧、九首人面龍身的人非人、飛廉、開明、烏獲和飛天；下部繪的是山林僧屋、走獸出没。僧屋內，僧人在静坐修行；僧屋外，走獸在山林中驚跑。這動與静的精彩對比場面，使全圖生動活潑，意境深遠雋永。

27. 第249窟　窟頂東披　力士捧摩尼寶珠
這個窟的塑像在清代時期重修，壁畫仍是西魏時期的原作。摩尼寶珠，即如意寶珠。據民間傳說："如得此寶珠者可隨意所求"。圖中部繪的是二力士捧蓮花摩尼寶珠；該力士手臂生翼，壯健有力。兩側繪有飛天，朱雀。下有胡人與烏獲現百戲和龜蛇相交的玄武及虎身人面九首的開明神獸等。此畫筆墨謹嚴，構圖疏密有

致，高矮錯落，動静結合，是一幅神道畫中的傳世佳作。

28. 第285窟　北壁上層　説法圖二鋪（七佛之五、六）
圖爲北壁上層東起第五鋪的拘那含牟尼佛和第六鋪的迦葉佛。二佛居中端坐，手施'無畏印'和'與願印'，目光下視，面稍帶微笑。二佛的上方華蓋左右各繪二飛天，其飛天姿態優美無比；佛的東西兩側各繪菩薩二身，其菩薩形體修長清秀；在兩佛的座位下方是墨書發願文，墨書發原文兩側繪的是供養人和供養人題記；其男供養人在右、女供養人在左。據第六鋪迦葉佛座下的發願文記載，此窟始建於大統四年（公元538年），可見這是本窟現存的最早紀年。

北周篇（公元 557—581 年）

29. 第296窟　窟頂北披西段　微妙再嫁梵志
這個窟在五代，清代時期重修。微妙再嫁梵志，是微妙比丘尼因緣中的一段故事，主要是描繪微妙前生'罪孽'，今世'報應'，后出家爲尼的艱辛苦難經歷。此畫是依據《賢愚經》第三卷《微妙比丘尼品十六》繪制而成的。故事説：微妙在産子之夜，丈夫醉酒回家，烹煮嬰兒，逼微妙吃下，微妙無奈，離家出走，途中與一新喪妻子上墳的長者結爲夫婦，但婚后不久，丈夫得病而死，微妙被殉葬。賊扒墳盜墓，微妙得救，賊又强逼微妙爲妻，賊被處死，微妙再次被殉葬；后又因狼扒墳而得救。最后繪微妙見佛，被剃度爲比丘尼。該畫內容豐富，情節曲折、生動、凄涼。作者把微妙今世的種種悲慘遭遇描繪的淋淋盡致，但同時也表露了她前生刺死嬰兒咎由自取、今世得到報應的結果；被譽爲敦煌石窟因緣故事畫中的代表作。

30. 第428窟　東壁南側　薩埵那太子本生
此窟在五代時期重修。本窟圖中薩埵那太子本生的繪制方法與北魏時期254窟不同的是：作者把壁畫平分爲上、中、下三段，成爲長卷式的構圖方式，并采用了畫史記載的"人大於山，水不溶泛"之技法，來突出人物和故事情節；各個情節分別繪三王子辭行、進山、遇虎，刺頸、投崖、飼虎、二兄報信、起塔供養；且每一情節均繪山、樹、屋爲間隔，自然形成了一幅緊密銜接的連環故事畫。畫中山石樹木、人與動物直現於眼前，讓人感到太子的慈善飼虎之舉，即悲壯又敬佩。

31. 第428窟　南壁　飛天與菩薩
圖中上部是四身半裸飛天，兩身在彈奏琵琶和箜篌，兩

身在舞蹈。下部是四身供養菩薩，一身著掩腋衣，手提净瓶，其余三身上半身皆裸體，下身均穿波斯褲，腰結蔽膝，披巾垂地；她們身姿相同，但手臂姿態各异。

32. 第432窟　中心柱東向面　龕外南側　脅侍菩薩

此窟在西夏時期重修。圖中的脅侍菩薩是西魏與北周期間塑造的，高1.22米，一手貼胸，一手下垂，披長巾，穿長裙，含笑俯視，神情歡悦。面腴頰豐，身材修長，飄逸俊美，色彩絢綺明麗，顯示了西魏和北周時期的審美時尚，被稱爲敦煌石窟彩塑的代表作。

33. 第428窟　東壁北側　須達拿太子本生

"須達拿太子本生"，屬本生故事畫之一，是依據西晋時期聖賢翻譯的《太子須達拿經》繪制而成的。其故事內容正如敦煌研究院樊錦詩院長所述："葉波國太子須達拿樂善好施，有求必應。敵國收買婆羅門，向他乞討百戰百勝的白象，太子慷慨相施。國王聞訊震怒，將須達拿驅逐出國。太子携妻、子驅馬車而去，一路上遇婆羅門乞討，遂將馬、車、衣物施舍殆盡，千辛萬苦來到遥遠的深山中隱居，結廬修行。后又來一婆羅門要他的兩個兒了，須達拿乘妻不在，以繩索縛二子交與婆羅門。最后婆羅門將孩子帶到葉波國出賣，爲國王知悉，將孫兒贖回，并迎太子回國。"全圖以上、中、下三層五十多個場面，詳細地描繪了葉波國須達拿太子樂施好善故事的全部過程；此畫格局縝密嚴謹，技法嫻熟老練，故事內容描繪豐富、曲折、生動、感同身受。

34. 第290窟　中心柱東向面上方　飛天

該窟在宋代時期重修，圖中四身飛天相向遨游在湛藍的天空中，周圍點綴著含苞待放的鮮花，這不僅使整個畫面得以均衡，更點醒了整個幅面的生氣。此畫用筆簡明粗獷，設色濃郁，像這樣的飛天在敦煌石窟中也實爲少見。

35. 第428窟　前室窟頂　人字披圖案

"人字披"圖案，即是人字形狀的圖案。在敦煌石窟北朝期間，多用這種圖案裝飾窟頂前后兩披。圖中繪大梁、檁條、椽子等，各椽子間彩繪蓮花化生、忍冬、瑞獸祥禽等紋樣。圖爲本窟前室頂的人字披圖案，也是敦煌石窟中最優秀的人字披圖案；圖案椽間裝飾忍冬、蓮荷，花草叢中還點綴着奔馳的鹿、飛翔的鳥、玩耍的猴等，真的是豐富多彩，生機盎然。

隋代篇（公元581—618年）

36. 第305窟　北壁下部　供養人

供養人，即是出資、籌資建窟的功德主，也稱窟主。在敦煌石窟中，男女供養人一般都在發願文榜題的左右兩側，即男在右，女在左，且左右均有比丘尼爲導引。而本圖的供養人與其他窟供養人却不雷同；因女供養人皆隨男供養人之后，其緣故待考。

37. 第419窟　西壁龕內　彩塑一鋪

此窟在西夏時期重修。圖爲本窟西壁龕內的一鋪塑像，佛端坐中央，二弟子二菩薩侍立左右。佛仰掌、施"無畏印"，形體豐滿，穿田相紋袈裟；弟子阿難聰慧、稚氣；迦葉衰老消瘦，但爽朗精練；菩薩端莊、典雅、秀美，五官刻劃洗練、輪廓清晰，亦屬隋代時期菩薩的代表作。

38. 第305窟　窟頂南披　西王母（帝釋天妃）

該窟是隋代開皇五年（公元585年）建造的，后在五代和清代時期重修。窟頂南披繪的是西王母乘四鳳駕車在彩雲中飛行：羽人馭車，車后旌旗飄蕩；比丘做導引，神獸爲護衛；飛天空中相隨。此畫設色深艷而不失典雅，畫面工而不滯、細而不膩，是隋時神道畫中之上品。

39. 第419窟　西壁龕內南側　脅侍菩薩與弟子阿難

此窟在西夏時期重修。圖爲龕內南側的兩身塑像—脅侍菩薩和弟子阿難。菩薩高1.81米，面相端莊秀美，右手下垂持净瓶，左手向上持柳枝。弟子阿難高1.65米，雙于托鉢，相貌少年俊秀。他們都是佛的近侍，但因道行等級不同，故他們的形體就有所別，一般菩薩的形體要比弟子大一些。

40. 第419窟　西壁龕內北側　脅侍菩薩與弟子迦葉

圖爲龕內北側的兩身塑像—菩薩和迦葉。此菩薩高1.81米，左手向上持柳枝，右手下垂提净瓶；面相清麗端莊，情態雍容優雅。弟子迦葉高1.65米，一手托鉢，一手握拳於嶙峋的胸前。此畫人物神態刻劃傳神入微，設色淡雅清秀，是敦煌石窟彩塑的代表作。

41. 第427窟　中心柱西向龕　弟子阿難

該窟在宋代時期重修。圖中的阿難高1.67米，是釋迦牟尼的十大弟子之一。他面目清秀，衣著檢樸，雙手合十，神情恭順地佇立在佛的右側，在聆聽釋迦牟尼佛說法。

42. 第420窟　窟頂東披　西域商隊

此窟在宋代、西夏時期重修。圖爲《法華經變之四·觀世音菩薩普門品》中的一部分。普門品即是"觀世音經"，主要描述觀音菩薩救苦救難和顯身普度衆生的各種情節。此圖便是其中一節，圖中繪一旅商隊牽著成群的駱駝，滿載貨物，跋涉重山峻嶺，受盡艱辛的情景。但不論路途是多麼的遥遠辛勞，艱險，遇到强盗，只要念誦觀世音菩薩的名號，便可化險爲夷。古代畫師們依據經文内容，繪出了圖中生動而有趣的畫面。如商隊在途中向神廟祈禱，爲牲口灌藥，牲口失足墜崖等。由於敦煌是舉世聞名的古代"絲綢之路"要道，又是往來客商的必經之地，故作者按照當時現實生活中所熟悉的人物、牲畜，創作出商隊長途跋涉、翻山越嶺的驚險圖景。因此，從這幅壁畫中使我們又看到了當年絲路古道的風采。

43. 第420窟　南向龕　彩塑一鋪

圖爲本窟南向龕内的塑像：一佛二菩薩。佛端坐在彩繪的獅子座上，作説法狀，形體高大厚實，神態莊嚴肅穆，身穿田相袈裟。侍立佛左右的二脅侍菩薩，一手提净瓶、一手持柳枝，相貌清雅端莊，比例匀稱；面部輪廓分明，眉、鼻、頤棱、轉折清晰，自然真實；服飾處理手法簡練，造型豐腴圓滿，色彩豐富華麗。古代藝術大師們的塑、繪熔爲一體的藝術創作，給工藝美術界作出了非凡貢獻。

44. 第420窟　西壁龕内北側　脅侍菩薩

图中的胁侍菩萨右手下垂提净瓶，左手握于胸前，神态端庄地立于莲花座上。他面相丰腴圆满，服饰处理手法简练，造型精美，色彩清新典雅，是敦煌石窟隋时最优秀的塑像之一。

45. 第420窟　西壁龕口南側　脅侍菩薩

請參見圖44第420窟南向龕《彩塑一鋪》文。

46. 第420窟　西壁龕口北側　脅侍菩薩

請參見圖44第420窟南向龕《彩塑一鋪》文

47. 第427窟　中心柱南向龕　弟子迦葉

圖中迦葉，修頭陀行，身體干瘦，雙手合十，虔誠恭順地佇立在佛的左側。他形容憔悴，滿面皺紋，但他的面部棱角分明，喉結突出，目光炯炯有神，顯示了老僧爽朗自信的風采。

48. 第57窟　南壁中央　説法圖

此窟在晚唐時期重修。説法圖正象敦煌研究院樊錦詩院長所考述的那樣：即"以佛爲主體，左右有脅侍菩薩、弟子、天龍八部護法、聽法，背景只有簡單的華蓋和樹木，或有蓮花水池。從畫面上無法判斷是什么佛，在什么時間、地點，針對什么對象的説法相，籠統地稱之這類壁畫題材爲説法圖；"但本圖不在此例。圖中阿彌陀佛端坐在華蓋、雙樹下的雙獅座上，觀世音菩薩和大勢至菩薩站立左右，合稱"西方三聖"。兩側有弟子迦葉，阿難和八大菩薩；前有雙獅守護，二力士護法，空有飛天散花。此畫構圖嚴謹，描繪精細，綫條流利酣暢，設色富麗，是初唐時期極爲珍貴的一幅上乘作品。

49. 第57窟　南壁中央《説法圖》東側　觀音菩薩

圖中的觀世音菩薩，是唐代菩薩形象中最負有盛名的代表作，譽有美人之稱，本窟也因此被國内外游客稱之爲"美人窟"。圖中的觀音菩薩容顏秀麗，肌膚潤澤細膩，體態嫻雅端莊；色彩深艷而不失典雅，描繪工整而不滯、細而不膩；特别是披巾和衣裙上的綫條，被刻劃的細致入微并精繪了各種花紋圖案，令人賞心悦目，同時也顯示了初唐時期的審美時尚。

50. 第57窟　北壁中央　説法圖

圖中央阿彌陀佛結跏趺坐於華蓋、菩提樹下的蓮花座上，迦葉、阿難、觀世音和大勢至菩薩侍立左右；碧綠的寶池水面上紅蓮綻開，綠意盎然的菩提樹旁飛天散花。此圖保存完整，筆法精致，風格隽秀。

51. 第57窟　北壁中央《説法圖》右側　大勢至菩薩

該菩薩形象姿容豐滿，儀態端莊、飄逸俊美，手執鮮花立於蓮化綻開的寶池之中。

52. 第71窟　北壁《阿彌陀經變》中　思維菩薩

該窟修建于初唐時期。圖爲佛陀座下的四尊思維菩薩，他們容貌姣妍，微低著頭，有的手托腮，有的手叉腰，有的雙手合十；濃黑的長眉下，一雙雙沉静恬淡的目光中好像悟出了真諦，生動地展現了菩薩神秘的心靈境界。

53. 第71窟　北壁　思維菩薩與供養菩薩

這是位於七十一窟北壁阿彌陀經變座下的兩身菩薩，

即一身思維菩薩和一身胡跪供養菩薩。思維菩薩盤腿而坐，右手撫膝、左手托腮，兩眼凝視空茫，嘴邊泛出一絲不易捉摸的微笑。胡跪供養菩薩頭偏轉，側臉，左手托供盤。此圖描繪精細，構思獨特，形象逼真，是敦煌石窟遺存的菩薩畫中、姿態最精美的一幅。

54. 第220窟　南壁《阿彌陀净土變》中　舞樂圖
此窟在中唐、晚唐、五代和清代時期重修。阿彌陀净土變也稱之西方净土變，屬敦煌佛教經變畫之一。本圖是西方净土變中一幅完整的大型舞樂場面，繪于唐貞觀十六年。圖中繪雙人對舞，舞者斜披天衣，頭戴寶冠、高髻，手握長巾，裙紗透體，面面相對，跣足在華麗的圓毯上翩翩起舞。據唐史籍記載，此舞叫"胡旋舞"。在"胡旋舞"兩側各繪樂隊一組，每組八人，演奏著箜篌、琵琶、笛子、筝、法螺等各種樂器；其場面聲勢浩大，宏偉壯觀，再現了當時宮庭中舞樂的盛況，是一幅極爲珍貴的音樂史料。

55. 第220窟　南壁　一佛二菩薩
圖中的阿彌陀佛身穿通肩袈裟，結跏趺坐於菩提樹下寶池之中的蓮花座上；寶池中綠水蕩漾，化生童子在水中嬉戲，觀世音和大勢至菩薩端莊地侍立左右，他們均是西方極樂世界之主人，合稱"西方三聖"。此畫色彩艷麗，人物造型優美，綫條流暢自然，是初唐時期不可多得的一幅珍希佳作。

56. 第220窟　北壁　藥師經變
此畫是依據《藥師琉璃光七佛本願功德經》繪制而成的；主要表現以藥師琉璃光佛爲主體的東方净土世界之七佛和琉璃世界之歌舞景象。在七佛下方，以燈樓爲中心，繪制了四人對舞的舞樂場面；東西兩側各繪一組樂隊，共二十八人組成：其東側十三人，西側十五人。除樂隊外，還有二菩薩正在燃點樹形七層藥師燈輪。在燈樓座下，有墨書的"貞觀十六年歲次壬寅奉爲大雲/寺律師道弘法師□奉□/……"的發願文，這是敦煌石窟初唐時期壁畫中的最早紀年。

57. 第401窟　北壁東側　供養菩薩
本窟建造于隋代，在初唐、五代、清代時期重修。圖爲北壁東側初唐時期繪制的一身供養菩薩。該菩薩左手執長巾，右手托玻璃供盤（玻璃在我國初唐時期爲最珍貴的寶器），神態瀟灑地立於蓮花座上。此畫描繪精致，綫條優美瀟脱，筆勢沉凝，著墨深郁，是一幅

不可多得的初唐時期珍品。

58. 第220窟　北壁《藥師净土變》東側　樂隊
圖爲《藥師净土變》東側的一組樂隊，其樂伎十三人正分別演奏著筝、簫、竪笛、方響、篳篥、阮咸、橫笛、腰鼓、都曇鼓、拍板、毛圓鼓等。他們膚色各异，但演奏神態專注，有主有次，章法井然，展現了當時宮庭樂隊演奏的真實情景。

59. 第220窟　東壁南側　維摩結
這是本窟東壁南側上部的維摩詰畫像。他手執拂塵坐於胡床之上，身體前傾，凝神斂眉，思慮深邃，胸有成竹。作者以流利剛健的綫描一氣呵成，給人有"虬須雲鬢，數尺飛動，毛根出肉，力健有余"之感。

60. 第220窟　東壁北側　帝王圖
該圖繪于唐貞觀十六年（公元642年），是維摩詰經變中的一部分；主要描繪經文"方便品"中的國王、大臣、諸王了官員等前去看望的場面。圖中帝王身高體胖，頭戴禮冠、并飾玉串，身穿青衣朱裳，氣宇軒昂，威武莊嚴，張開雙臂，在群臣的簇擁下昂首闊步而行。此畫綫描流利挺勁，設色濃艷華麗，暈染柔和細膩，體現了作者精熟、高超的繪畫技藝。

61. 第321窟　西壁龕頂南側　菩薩赴會
這個窟在五代，清代時期重修。圖中飛天在蔚藍的天空中自由翱翔；六身體態婀娜多姿的菩薩乘彩雲前來赴會，在天宮樓臺上倚欄觀賞著下界眾生，他們指點著、議論著，氣氛和諧歡快，意趣盎然。

62. 第322窟　南壁　説法圖
該窟在五代時期重修。這幅説法圖爲彌勒説法圖，圖中主尊善跏倚坐在菩提華蓋之下，衆菩薩脅侍左右，其菩薩身姿秀麗，服飾簡略，設色富麗而不艷，是初唐時期一種淡雅的繪畫風格。

63. 第322窟　東壁門上方《説法圖》中　菩薩
這是東壁門上方説法圖中的菩薩。此菩薩盤腿正面坐於蓮花座上，頭稍斜，左手握花，右手捻帶，雙眼微睜下視，沉静恬淡；繪制技法精工嚴整，用筆輕柔飄灑，設色清淡，趣味雅致。

64. 第322窟　西壁龕内北側　天王與菩薩
請參見圖65《彩塑一鋪》文。

65. 第322窟　西壁龕内南側　彩塑一鋪

此龕内共有塑像七身，但本圖只是龕内、居中部位的釋迦佛和南側的弟子阿難、菩薩及天王四身塑像。其釋迦佛高1.76米，頤圓額寬、高鼻梁、平胸挺腰，身穿袈裟，神情莊嚴地趺坐於蓮臺上。阿難高1.60米，衣著檢樸，虔誠地侍立佛側。菩薩裸上身，斜披天衣，左手上舉，神情安祥，儀態端莊地立於蓮花座上。天王高1.50米，兩手已殘，濃眉大眼，鼻挺唇厚，虬鬚突出，身披長巾穿盔甲，由長靴護腿，腳踏地神，威風凜凜。

66. 第329窟　窟頂　蓮花飛天藻井

蓮花飛天藻井，是藻井圖案的一種。圖爲第329窟初唐時期所繪的一幅蓮花飛天藻井圖案。此圖案繪製精美，筆法方折細挺，疏密有致；整個畫面五彩繽粉，氣氛活潑，色彩富麗堂皇，特別是那環繞蓮花井心飛翔的四身飛天，其容顏嬌媚，姿態婀娜，瀟灑地在蔚藍的'天空'中回旋、流動，長巾隨白雲飄舞，并被譽稱爲初唐時期藻井圖案的代表作品。

67. 第329窟　東壁南側　女供養人

這個窟在五代和清代時期重修。圖爲本窟東壁南側《説法圖》下初唐時期所繪製的一身女供養人畫像。這身女供養人體態豐盈綽約，端莊恬靜，頭束髻，穿窄袖小衫，圓領露胸，系長裙，手持蓮花，跪在毯子上目視前方。作者用寫實的手法，完美地塑造了一個貴族婦女的虔誠和雍容華貴之態，是一幅不可多得的刻畫唐時貴族婦女内心深處活動的稀世珍品。

68. 第329窟　西壁龕頂南側　夜半逾城

圖爲佛教故事中的一個情節：描繪悉達多太子十九歲時感到人世間有諸多的生、老、病、死等苦惱，意決出家修道，以求解脱的情景。一日夜半，乘馬逾出迦毗羅衛城。圖中太子頭戴寶冠，乘馬在雲中奔越，前有乘龍天人開道，后有天女、力士護衛，諸伎樂飛天在彩雲中隨行奏樂散花，還有祥雲瑞氣，使得整個畫面花團錦族，五彩繽紛；再現了佛祖出家修道的感人一幕。

69. 第321窟　東壁北側　十一面觀音

十一面觀音，也稱大光普照觀音，是六觀音之一。該觀音十一面六臂，裙紗透體，一手下垂提净瓶，一手上舉持柳枝，神情莊静地立於雙樹下的蓮花座上。二菩薩侍立左右，其姿態嫵媚婀娜。此畫保存完整，布局縝密嚴謹，左右對稱；用筆流暢細致，綫描柔中露剛，細勁曲折，技法嫻熟老練，確是唐代的名手之筆。

70. 第220窟　北壁《藥師經變》西側　伎樂

圖爲本窟北壁《藥師經變》西側樂隊中的一個樂工。此樂工雙手抱螺，凝神專注的在演奏。從他使用的樂器上看，顯然是南方的濱海民族。作者通過對樂工形態、相貌、和樂器的描繪手法，含蓄地表現了人物的民族特征。此畫人物神態刻劃傳神入微，畫面構圖起伏循環，設色雅致，格調超逸。

71. 第321窟　西壁龕頂南側　雙飛天

據佛經記載，飛天是"乾達婆"和"緊那羅"二神的衍變，常飛行在佛國的霓雲彩霧的天空之中，屬天龍八部之一。乾達婆是古印度神話中的歌神，傳説他的相貌非常英俊、瀟灑；緊那羅是古印度神話中的樂神，顯現女身時爲乾達婆之妻。圖爲莫高窟第321窟西壁龕頂南側初唐時期繪製的二身飛天。該飛天造型優美，綫條流利酣暢，體態輕盈瀟灑，神韵怡人，是初唐時期飛天佳作之中的上品。

72. 第57窟　西壁龕内南側　菩薩

圖爲第57窟西壁龕内主尊佛像南側的一身菩薩塑像：該菩薩右手下垂握净瓶，左手上抬托蓮花，神態恬静，跣足立於佛側。他的造像形態雖不如盛唐時期菩薩的嫵媚優雅，但也略顯出女性化的文静和優美，因此時的造像技藝正是由隋代雕塑藝術向盛唐雕塑藝術轉變的過渡時期。

盛唐期（公元712—781年）

73. 第45窟　西壁龕内北側　菩薩（局部）

這身裊娜玉婷的唐塑菩薩，是敦煌石窟塑像中、形態最美最有特色的一尊。其高1.85米；頭戴寶冠、束高髻，臉形渾圓飽滿，裸上身、胸飾瓔珞，身穿團花錦繡羅裙，披巾斜挂於胸前，肌膚玉潔冰清，體態輕盈、嬌繞嫵媚，是一尊不可多得的稀世珍品。

74. 第45窟　西壁龕内北側　迦葉・菩薩・天王

該窟始建於初唐時期，在中唐、五代時期重修。圖爲四十五窟西壁龕内北側的迦葉、菩薩、天王三身塑像。其迦葉高1.75米，老成持重，襟懷坦蕩；菩薩高1.85米，翠眉秀目，神態輕盈嫵媚；天王高1.79米，兩眼怒視前方，雄健威武。他們雖性情身份各異而却渾然一體，這三身塑像是敦煌石窟盛唐時期最優秀的作品，也是敦煌石窟彩塑的代表。

75. 第45窟　南壁　西側　商人遇盜圖

圖爲‘觀音普門品’中商人遇盜的一個故事場面。有一群商人趕着毛驢，駄著絲綢、珠寶，途經山野之中，被三名强盜持刀劫奪，諸商人無奈從牲口背上卸下貨物。圖中商人的恐慌，毛驢的竪耳長鳴，强盜的持刀劫奪，山野崗坡的雜草樹林，皆被描繪得淋漓盡致，生動地再現了古絲路經商途中的艱險實情。

76. 第45窟　北壁　觀無量壽經變（全）

觀無量壽經變是觀無量壽佛經變的略稱。《觀無量壽經》是梵文經典的譯名。（《觀無量壽經》中國三國時期已早有漢文譯本，共有三本，但現僅遺存姜良耶舍一本）。此圖以西方净土爲中心，東西兩側以“未生怨”與“十六觀”竪長條平面畫形成三聯式結構圖。圖中央阿彌陀佛結跏趺坐在蓮花座上說法，兩側衆菩薩在聽法，下部平臺兩側的樂隊在演奏，二舞伎在翩翩起舞，是一派歌舞升平的西方極樂世界。作者把佛的面目慈祥，菩薩的凝神静聽，舞樂的歡快，殿堂樓閣的壯麗，描繪得熱烈、祥和、美麗，真是令人神往。

77. 第23窟　北壁西側　雨中耕作圖

該窟的壁畫，在中唐、五代時期重繪，彩塑在清代時期重修。圖爲《法華經變·藥草喻品》中的一個雨中耕作場面。空中烏雲密布，陰雨綿綿，雨中的田野到處是一片片翠田綠地，田間莊稼、藥草茂盛，農夫有的挑擔，有的在雨中扶犁耕田；一農婦到田頭送飯。作者以田園生活的筆觸，把古代農民在雨中奮力耕作的喜悦情景，描繪得生氣勃勃，真真切切。

78. 第39窟　西壁龕頂　飛天

此窟在五代、西夏、清代時期重修。圖中飛天祥雲托體，雙手捧花盤由空中俯衝而降。飛天的長裙和披巾以雜彩圖案爲花飾，在彩雲的襯托下，更顯得五色斑斕，分外絢麗。此飛天臉部和軀體均已脫色，但他的姿態優美，綫條描繪遒勁流暢，色彩典雅仍清晰可見，是敦煌石窟最有特色的飛天之一。

79. 第79窟　西壁龕內　彩塑一鋪

此窟在五代時期重修。圖爲七十九號窟西壁盝頂帳形龕內的一鋪彩塑：此鋪彩塑共有塑像九身，即一佛、四菩薩、二弟子、二天王。龕內佛像居中，善跏坐，短額頤豐，右手上舉作“說法印”，身著田相袈裟，面神略現笑容。四菩薩裸上身，披巾斜挂；二弟子跣足，虔敬地立於佛側，天王像臂壯胸闊，威風凛凛地立於龕外兩側。此鋪彩塑保存完整，布局相應對稱，人物造型“豐肌膩體”，色彩濃郁艷麗，雖經后代重修，但仍不失唐代塑像藝術之風彩。

80. 第130窟　西壁　大佛（局部）

莫高窟第130窟始建於盛唐時期，在宋代時期重修。圖中大佛是莫高窟兩大佛之一，譽稱第二大佛（《莫高窟記》中稱南大佛），高26米，塑造於公元713年－721年間（即唐開元九年前后），爲善跏坐彌勒佛像。此佛像氣度包容萬物，氣勢恢宏磅礴，威嚴肅穆。

81. 第148窟　東壁南側　觀無量壽經變（全）

這是在晚唐、西夏、清代三個時期重修的洞窟。圖爲敦煌石窟最大的一幅經變畫，此畫以西方净土世界爲中心，未生怨和十六觀繪於其中心兩側；無量壽佛居中、結跏趺坐於華蓋下的蓮花座上說法，觀音和大勢至菩薩等聖衆脅侍左右。水池上起平臺中部二舞伎正在表演，兩側樂隊爲其伴奏；臺下水池綠波蕩漾，化生童子坐于蓮花中嬉戲。該畫面上部繪的是宮殿、亭臺、樓閣，屬宮庭建築，其規模龐大，恢宏壯觀，體現了盛唐建築特色的精典。此畫構圖氣勢雄偉，用筆蒼勁嫻熟，工整嚴謹，細致穩健，是極爲珍貴的宮庭建築研究史料。

82. 第130窟　甬道南壁　都督夫人太原王氏供養像

圖爲都督夫人携眷屬禮佛的情景。該大人雍容華貴，身穿紅裙，肩巾垂足，雙手攏袖虔誠地立於華蓋下的花毯上，榜題爲“都督夫人太原王氏一心供養”；身穿綠長裙、手持鮮花和身着黄色長裙、雙手攏袖者是王氏二女，榜題爲“女十一娘一心供養”；“女十三娘一心供養”；身穿男裝的九名侍者緊隨其后。此圖人物形象姿容豐滿，神態端莊生動，色彩艷麗，清新明快，是敦煌石窟僅有的一幅稀世珍品。

83. 第172窟　南壁　觀無量壽經變（全）

此窟始建於盛唐時期，在宋代、清代重修。這是本窟南壁的一巨幅《觀無量壽經變》全圖，正中央三座大殿有配殿、角樓、塔式圓亭，并於虹橋相連。無量壽佛身穿田相袈裟，端坐於殿前中央華蓋之下的蓮花座上説法，其神態莊嚴肅穆；觀音、大勢至等諸菩薩左右聽法，殿前二舞伎，在翩翩起舞；兩側樂隊，在爲之伴奏。寶池中綠水蕩漾，蓮荷顯現，鴛鴦嬉戲，特別是那樓臺亭閣隱匿在綠樹青水之中的含蓄隽永，使整個畫面更顯得境界深邃，宏偉壯觀。

84. 第 172 窟　北壁　觀無量壽經變（全）
無量壽佛結跏趺坐於殿前中央菩提華蓋之下的蓮花座上，雖面部已脱色、毀壞，但仍能顯出他包容萬物的氣度和莊嚴；脅侍左右的大小諸菩薩有的在聽法，有的作思維之狀。殿前兩側樂師正在演奏，仙鶴在長鳴，空中飛天在翱翔。池中綠荷浮水，紅蓮嬌艷，鴛鴦嬉戲，化生童子悠游其間；這種祥和歡樂的獨特意境，充滿著佛國生活的真趣。

85. 第 172 窟　北壁東側 十六觀中　日想觀
"日想觀"，爲《觀無量壽經變》中十六觀的第一觀。圖中碧綠的河水，衝洗著赭色的山石崖壁；遠處落日西沉，但夕陽余暉仍映得崖壁如血；近處樹木稀疏、落葉飄零。韋提希夫人手執熏爐跪在潺潺流水的崖下河邊，觀望著漸入陰霾的紅日。此畫景致甚是蕭瑟，但日落的余暉，却又點破了整個畫面的冷寂。

86. 第 217 窟　北壁　觀無量壽經變（全）
此窟在晚唐、五代、清代三個時期重修。本圖是敦煌壁畫中最富麗堂皇的一幅觀無量壽經變，特別是那豪華的宮庭建築更是氣勢磅礴、宏偉壯觀；那靈鷲山佛的説法、衆菩薩聽法的精彩場面、樂隊的演奏、二舞伎的舞蹈、空中飛天散花的美姿，生動地展現了極樂世界的奇景盛況。此畫廣闊浩大，筆勢沉凝，色彩富麗明快，與濃郁的宮苑豪氣，再現了中國盛唐時期卓越精湛的繪畫藝術和獨特的建築藝術風格。

87. 第 217 窟　北壁《觀無量壽經變》東側　坐佛與菩薩
這是繪在《觀無量壽經變》圖中央下部的"阿彌陀净土"中佛與菩薩。此佛莊嚴肅穆盤腿坐於蓮花座上；因佛身已變爲紅綜色，被譽稱"紫磨金身"。菩薩容貌姣媚俊秀，神態莊静地立於佛旁聽法。此畫墨綫濃淡結合，運筆熟練、精細，是唐時最優秀的一幅作品。

88. 第 217 窟　北壁西側《觀無量壽經變》中　阿彌陀佛
圖中的阿彌陀佛，兩眼前視，端坐於蓮花座上。上有飛天菩提寶蓋，兩側有四菩薩脅侍。該畫施色濃艷華麗，構圖左右對稱，縝密嚴謹；畫風工整細膩，技法

嫻熟老練，反映了唐時審美的藝術風格。

89. 第 217 窟　南壁西側　化城喻品
圖爲法華經變中一段化城喻品的故事場面。故事説：有一群人，在導師的陪同下，到遥遠的地方去取寶，途中經艱險惡路，曠無人烟之地，衆人皆疲備恐懼；正在危難欲退之機，導師靈機一變，化爲一城，讓衆人休息，并鼓勵衆人繼續前往。此圖以幾個場景進行描繪，中間右下導師裸上身著短裙，赤足前邊導引，后者二騎跟隨。畫中山巒逶嶂，綠草如茵，古樹點綴着山脊和峽谷，并有河流蜿蜒，頗有濃郁的民族風情意味。

90. 第 217 窟　西壁龕頂　説法圖（局部）
該圖主要描繪的是：釋迦佛爲四衆説法和携衆弟子回到伽毗羅衛城探母的兩個精彩畫面。此幅畫構圖有致，取舍得體；人物造型准確、并富有生氣；用筆勁健，色彩絢爛無比，是唐時壁畫中色彩保存最佳的一幅。

91. 第 217 窟　西壁龕内北側　比丘
圖爲唐畫中不多見的一幅比丘畫像。他身穿袈裟、濃眉大眼、深深的皺紋，臉帶笑容，一幅驚奇而又歡欣的樣子立於蓮花臺上。此畫設色濃麗，筆調雅致，人物形象逼真，真實地顯現了唐時風韵。

92. 第 320 窟　南壁《阿彌陀經變》上部　雙飛天
這個窟在中唐、宋代、元代時期重修。在敦煌壁畫中有"無處不飛天"之稱。圖中的四身飛天、相對而飛，一身在飛翔散花，一身追逐、嬉戲相隨；真是惟肖惟妙，盡善盡美。此畫用筆蒼勁，墨韵酣暢，色彩艷麗，實爲飛天畫中之神品。

93. 第 328 窟　西壁龕内佛壇　彩塑一鋪
此鋪彩塑原爲九身，現存只有八身：因龕内南側外端一身供養菩薩于一九二四年被美國華爾納盜走（今陳列在美國波士頓博物館）。龕内中央是唐塑佛像中保存比較完整的一身，其高 2.19 米，正襟危坐，莊嚴肅穆。龕内北側的半跏菩薩像：連座高 1.87 米，南側的半跏菩薩像：連座高 1.90 米。他們一腿盤曲，一腿下垂，作"游戲座"式。其體態豐盈，氣度高雅。南側的弟子阿難：高 1.83 米，年輕聰穎，兩手籠袖扭腰。北側的弟子迦葉：高 1.80 米，雙手合十，沉穩謙恭。龕内北側的供養菩薩：高 1.12 米，神有所思，胡跪於蓮臺之上。龕外南側、北側的胡跪供養菩薩：高 1 米，其文静，虔誠。這些精美的塑像，藝術造詣精深，是敦煌石窟唐

時塑像的最杰出代表。

94. 第328窟　西壁龕内中央　坐佛
　　這是塑在本窟西壁龕中央的一身坐佛：高2.19米，正襟危坐，莊嚴肅穆。佛的衣折、垂裙、頂光、背光、項光和佛座，皆被技藝高超的匠師們用各種色彩妝扮的金碧輝爛，豐富多彩。

95. 第328窟　西壁龕内北側　半跏菩薩
　　請參閱93圖第328窟《彩塑一鋪》文。

96. 第328窟　西壁龕内北側　半跏菩薩（局部）
　　請參閱93圖第328窟《彩塑一鋪》文。

97. 第328窟　西壁龕内南側　半跏菩薩
　　請參閱93圖第328窟《彩塑一鋪》文。

98. 第328窟　西壁龕内北側　迦葉與菩薩
　　請參閱93圖第328窟《彩塑一鋪》文。

99. 第328窟　西壁龕内南側　阿難與菩薩
　　請參閱93圖第328窟《彩塑一鋪》文。

100. 第328窟　西壁龕内南側　弟子阿難（局部）
　　請參閱93圖第328窟《彩塑一鋪》文。

101. 第328窟　西壁龕内北側　供養菩薩
　　請參閱93圖第328窟《彩塑一鋪》文。

102. 第328窟　西壁龕内北側　供養菩薩（局部）
　　請參閱93圖第328窟《彩塑一鋪》文。

103. 第328窟　西壁龕外北側　供養菩薩
　　請參閱93圖第328窟《彩塑一鋪》文。

104. 第328窟　西壁龕外南側　供養菩薩
　　請參閱93圖第328窟《彩塑一鋪》文。

中唐篇（公元781—818年）

105. 第112窟　南壁東側《觀無量壽經變》中　反彈琵琶
　　該窟在宋代和清代時期重修。"反彈"是奏樂時的一種姿勢，"琵琶"是樂器的一種。圖爲阿彌陀佛座前的一個舞樂場面。舞者高髻寶冠，上身半裸，腰束帶，披長巾，回手撥弦，背身反彈琵琶，踏足而舞，其舞姿優美、神韻怡人。作者以嫻熟的筆觸繪出了舞者爐火純青的技藝，也展現了唐時舞蹈藝術的高超。

106. 第25窟（榆林窟）　南壁　觀無量壽經變（全）
　　榆林窟，地方俗稱萬佛峽，位於今甘肅省安西縣城西南七十公裏處的榆林河（也叫踏石河）東、西兩岸的崖壁上，現存各時代洞窟四十二個，壁畫四千二百平方米，彩塑二百五十九身，是敦煌石窟莫高窟以外的最大一處石窟群。此處壁畫，内容豐富，并繪制十分精美，有綠壁畫之稱。圖106，爲榆林窟第二十五窟南壁中唐時期所繪制的一鋪"觀無量壽經變"畫。此畫與莫高窟唐時前期壁畫題材相同，采納"三聯式"結構，即中央是大幅的阿彌陀净土，東、西兩側是豎長條平面畫"未生怨"和"十六觀"。圖中的"極樂世界"不像其他的净土畫那樣有衆多的人物，而是按畫面的實際大小、安排了適當數目的人物形象，使整個畫面更顯得清新疏朗。畫中的綠水、綠地、綠樹葉，還有那紅欄、紅柱、紅袈裟，把此鋪的經變畫妝扮得華麗多彩，燦爛輝煌。

107. 第25窟（榆林窟）　南壁《觀無量壽經變》東側　大勢至菩薩
　　本窟始建於中唐，后經五代、宋代、清代、三個時期重修。圖中的大勢至菩薩，位於本窟南壁《觀無量壽經變》圖東側；身穿紅裙，披長巾，手持法器，跣足立在蓮花臺上。此畫作者運用了流利勁健的鐵綫描勾勒，淡彩敷色，暈染柔和細膩，動態處理自然大方。

108. 第25窟（榆林窟）　南壁《觀無量壽經變》西側　觀世音菩薩
　　這是繪在本窟南壁《觀無量壽經變》圖西側的一身觀世音菩薩像。此觀音菩薩身穿白色長裙，左手持净瓶，右手持柳枝，壯静地立於蓮花臺上。該幅圖的綫描勾勒、施色、暈染、人物動態處理，皆和本窟107圖相同。

109. 第158窟　西壁壇上　卧佛
　　此窟開鑿於公元780年之后的吐蕃統治時期，是敦煌石窟最著名的涅槃窟之一。圖爲本窟西壁前佛壇上巨大的一尊石胎泥塑涅槃像，全長15.80米，僅頭部就有3米左右。據佛經記載，釋迦佛仙逝時應："即於是夜，右脅而卧，汩然大寂"。從卧佛的整個神態來看：他右脅而卧，面含微笑，自然、放松、超脱和美麗，這確已表現了"寂滅爲樂"的涅槃境界。

110. 第158窟　北壁涅槃變中　各國王子舉哀
　　據《大般涅槃經》記載：釋迦佛涅槃時，各國帝王、王子等前往拘尸那城哀悼。此圖即是各國帝王、王子前來舉哀的生動場面。赴釋迦涅槃舉哀的（以人物的服飾、相貌、膚色區分）有：吐蕃贊普和漢族帝王，還有突厥、回鶻、南海昆侖、中亞、南亞等國的王子。他們個個悲痛欲絕，因他們來自於不同民族和地區，所以哀悼表達的方式也不同；他們的有的割耳、鼻，有的挖心、剖腹，有的嚎啕大哭，有的悲泣等。這種哀哭喧鬧的場面，更加襯托了佛的寧靜和安詳，同時也體現了各民族的喪俗特質。

111. 第158窟　西壁龕頂　持瓔珞飛天
這身彩雲環繞，手持瓔珞的飛天，雙目凝視下方，衣飾飄帶隨風飛舞，朝著已入涅槃的釋迦佛徐徐而降；像是朝著已入涅槃之境的釋迦佛虔誠供養。該飛天，綫條流利酣暢，造型精美，姿態婀娜，色彩典雅，是唐時飛天之上品。

112. 第158窟　西壁龕頂　吹笛飛天
請參見111圖本窟龕頂《持瓔珞飛天》文。

113. 第159窟　東壁南側　吐蕃贊普與各國王子
這是本窟東壁南側"維摩詰經變"中吐蕃贊普與各國王子聽法的一個場面。圖中的吐蕃贊普，身穿翻領長袖大衫，腰束帶、項飾瑟瑟珠，頭戴紅氈高帽，佩腰刀，穿烏靴，右手執香爐，左手長袖及地，氣宇不凡地立於華蓋之下。前有二侍者導行，后有穿著不同民族服飾的各國王子簇擁。畫家以洗練生動的筆觸對不同身份、氣質、儀態的人物形象進行精心刻劃塑造，把其中人與人之間的相互關系處理得吻合、得體、到位，客觀地展現了吐蕃轄領沙洲時期與周邊國家睦鄰友好關系。這幅出色的作品，不僅體現了畫家有出眾的繪畫才能，同時也反映了畫家對重要歷史人物的高度讚許。

114. 第159窟　東壁南側　吐蕃贊普
請參閱113圖《吐蕃贊普與各國王子》文。

115. 第15窟（榆林窟）　前室頂南端　吹笛飛天
此窟在宋、西夏、元、清時期重修，但前室頂南端所繪制的飛天仍是中唐時期的原作。圖中的飛天：面容豐腴，裸上身，披長巾，頭戴寶冠，項飾瓔珞；兩手持笛接唇在空中吹奏，其飄帶隨彩雲漫卷，裙裾隨風飄曳，意態瀟灑、優美，神韵怡人，是唐時杰出的代表作品。

116. 第159窟　南壁中央　觀無量壽經變
這是中唐時期遺存最完整的一幅巨型經變畫，它和初、盛唐時期所繪制的"觀無量壽經變"內容，布局，構圖同屬一脉。圖中的無量壽佛説法、諸菩薩聽法、樂隊奏樂、舞伎揮巾相對起舞，樓臺高閣、綠荷浮水、紅蓮盛開無不被畫家描繪的惟妙惟肖。此畫構圖嚴謹，人物組合疏密得當，畫風樸實自然，用筆蒼勁雄健，設色秀潤雅逸。

117. 第159窟　西壁南側　普賢變
普賢變是敦煌佛教經變畫之一，也是與文殊變相對稱的題材畫。圖為第159窟西壁南側吐蕃時期繪制的一鋪普賢變：圖中的普賢菩薩，衣冠楚楚，右手撫膝，左手托玻璃花鉢，半跏坐於白象背上的蓮花座上，一奴僕手牽白象，另一奴僕雙手扶供盤頂於頭上，諸菩薩聖衆前呼后擁地行在雲海之中。畫中山川秀水參差錯落、婆娑多姿，真是情景交融，華麗多彩；不愧爲敦煌藝術之精品。

118. 第159窟　西壁龕內南側　天王、菩薩、阿難
這是一組中唐時期最精美的彩塑。圖中的天王竪眉瞪眼，身披鎧甲，體態魁偉，神態強悍；菩薩像高1.39米，身軀稍傾斜，上穿小花衲衣，下著茶花羅裙，面相豐腴，神態端莊；阿難高1.30米，眉清目秀，裙襦華麗，舉止瀟灑，意態莊靜、慈厚。此鋪彩塑造型精美，色彩清新淡雅，是敦煌石窟中唐時期彩塑中的佳作。

119. 第159窟　西壁龕內北側　迦葉、菩薩、天王
圖中弟子迦葉高1.30米，身穿衲衣，白色的長裙上彩繪著精美的葉形圖案，右肩袒露，臉含微笑。菩薩高1.38米，相貌端正，黛眉朱唇，亭亭玉立地站於蓮花臺上。天王兩手掌上托，挺胸，精神抖擻，威嚴勇猛。這二柔一剛，一靜一動，三者相得益彰。

120. 第18窟（西千佛洞）　西壁　觀無量壽經變
敦煌西千佛洞第18窟建造于中唐時期，在宋代重修。該圖描繪的是阿彌陀佛、西方諸聖和極樂淨土的美好場景。此圖格局縝密嚴謹，技法嫻熟老練，敷色豐富艷麗；畫面氣勢雄渾，宏偉壯觀，是中唐時期西千佛洞遺存最完整的一幅稀世珍品。

121. 第18窟（西千佛洞）　南壁西側　不空羂索觀音
不空羂索觀音：不空：顧名思義，即必有所獲；羂索：

在佛教中指佛、菩薩管束眾生的法器。圖爲敦煌石窟群之一的西千佛洞第18窟、南壁西側吐蕃時期所繪制的一幅不空羂索觀音,此觀音面相秀麗,項戴羂索,端莊地坐於華蓋下的蓮花座上;諸菩薩和眷屬環繞四周。畫中綫條流暢,人物體態優美,設色豐富雅致,是唐風時尚完美的表現。

122. 第16窟(西千佛洞) 窟頂南披 説法圖(回鶻)

西千佛洞,位於甘肅省敦煌市西南約三十五公裏處的黨河北岸斷崖上,屬敦煌石窟群之一,是敦煌石窟藝術的重要組成部分。現存各時期洞窟二十二個;即北魏二個,北朝一個,西魏一個,北周四個,隋代三個,初唐三個,中唐一個,晚唐三個,五代二個,回鶻一個,元代一個。本圖第十六窟始建於晚唐時期,后在五代、宋代、回鶻時期重修。圖爲回鶻時期所繪的一鋪説法圖,該圖保存完整,人物繪制精美,綫條流利酣暢,色彩清新淡雅,是敦煌石窟回鶻時期的優秀作品。

123. 第18窟(西千佛洞) 窟頂南披 説法圖與千佛

説法圖四周繪千佛在敦煌石窟中是司空見慣的常用布局格式。圖爲西千佛洞窟頂南披吐蕃時期繪制的一鋪説法圖:畫中佛結跏趺坐在菩提華蓋下的蓮花座上,二供養菩薩跪于香案兩側,諸千佛坐於蓮花座上作'定印'。畫中粗放豪邁的勁綫勾勒,畫風樸實、沉著,構圖獨特新穎,敷色典雅,反映了唐時的審美情趣。

晚唐篇(公元848—907年)

124. 第14窟 窟頂 藻井

此窟始建於晚唐,后在宋、清時期重修。本窟的窟頂藻井圖案與其他藻井圖案相形不同之處:就是在井心畫兩個十字相父的"金剛杆"(金剛杵,是佛教密宗的一種降魔法器,繪在藻井圖案中有降魔的宗教含義。);四披各繪四方佛赴會説法相一鋪,井外邊飾、垂幔皆與一般的藻井相同。像此類藻井圖案在敦煌石窟中遺存甚少,敷彩也十分淡雅,描繪工整細膩,構圖簡潔達意,不失爲唐時佳作。

125. 第12窟 北壁 藥師經變

這個窟建於咸通十年(公元869年),但在五代、清代時期重修;窟中的部分壁畫已於五代時期重繪,但此幅經變畫乃晚唐時期原作。藥師經變是東方藥師淨土變的略稱。本圖中央繪的是藥師佛,手持藥鉢,端莊地坐於樂音樹下的蓮花臺上,給諸菩薩、弟子、國王大臣、天龍八部,十二藥叉大將説《藥師琉璃光如來本願功德經》。此畫構圖疏中有密、静中有動,人物神態刻劃精細;因圖下方有榜題"東方藥師淨土變",故稱此圖爲藥師經變畫。

126. 第12窟 前室西壁北側 天王

此天王稱北方天王毗沙門,又叫多聞天,是佛教護法的四大天王之一。他頭戴翼冠,鎧甲戎裝,一手持棒,一手托塔,威風凜凜。據佛經記載,毗沙門天王居住在須彌山的半山腰之北方,爲北方天主,所以人們稱他爲北方天王。該畫繪制精細,施色雅致,爲晚唐天王像的代表作。

127. 第12窟 南壁西端 作戰圖

這是一幅描繪古代兩陣對壘的戰爭精彩畫面,是依據法華經變安樂行品中的"髻珠喻"故事繪制而成的。作戰圖是安樂行品的別稱,圖中兩國軍隊正在交戰:一方軍隊冒著矢箭躍馬橫衝,另一方軍隊正張弓射箭在河邊迎敵。河中人仰馬翻,尸橫遍野。作者抓住了戰爭高潮的一瞬間,以超凡的概括筆觸,繪出了兩國交戰的生動場面,仿佛使人有身臨其境之感。此畫構圖嚴謹,筆調洗練,言簡意賅,是研究中國唐代戰爭史的珍貴史料。

128. 第17窟 北壁 高僧像—洪䛒

這就是著名的藏經洞,建于大中五年(公元851年),洞裏封存了數萬件經卷、文書、絹畫等。它發現於公元1900年(清光緒二十六年)。窟門開在第16窟甬道的北壁,比第16窟地面高出1米,圖中的洪䛒高僧塑像、原存放在其中。該塑像高94厘米,盤腿、結跏趺坐,雙手置於腹前,作禪定狀,身著通肩袈裟,面相飽滿,鼻隆頤豐,兩眼炯炯有神。從相貌上看,像是一位學者似的高僧。此塑像,是敦煌石窟遺存唯一的一尊高僧寫真像。

129. 第17窟 北壁西側 近事女

近事女,唐代以前稱"優婆夷",是在家受五戒修行,專門侍奉高僧的女子。圖中的近事女畫像繪在洪䛒高僧塑像右側的墻壁上,她身穿男裝,面頰豐圓,眉清目秀,容貌端莊,右手握杖,左手托長巾,立於枝葉茂盛的菩提樹下。此畫筆法工細而具力度，綫條輕松而飄逸，人物神態傳神而生動，是一幅難得的唐時人物畫上品。

130. 第17窟　北壁東側　比丘尼
圖中的供養比丘尼畫像位于第17窟北壁洪䛒高僧塑像的東側：他身穿袈裟，手持雙龍圖案的團扇，立於菩提樹下。樹上挂着僧人用的净水瓶，兩只小鳥正向枝葉繁茂的菩提樹飛去。該畫描繪工整細膩，色彩豐富典雅；兩只相互追逐的小鳥、不僅使畫面得以均衡，却更點醒了整個畫面的生氣。

131. 第9窟　南壁　擊鼓外道
這個窟由張承奉建造于大順元年間（即公元890—893年）；后經宋、元、清三個時期重修。圖中舍利弗與勞度叉鬥法的故事場面，是據《賢愚經·須達起精舍緣品》繪制而成的。故事説：勞度叉化作一樹，枝葉繁茂；舍利弗化出旋風，吹樹拔根，鼓傾架倒，使蛇無處藏，外道六師無法擊鼓，節節敗退，最后舍利弗獲勝，外道六師只好剃度出家，皈依佛門。

132. 第85窟　窟頂東披　楞伽經變
此窟由翟法榮建造於唐咸通年間（公元860—874年），后經五代、元代、清代期間重修。圖中的楞伽經變畫，是據《大乘入楞伽經》繪制而成的；主要是描繪釋迦佛在楞伽城説法的一個場面。圖中心繪的是楞伽佛會，描述楞伽城主人羅婆那王邀請釋迦佛入城中説法的情景。兩側繪的是大小不等的説法圖，并藉於榜題文字給以闡釋。此圖内容豐富，段落分明，結構嚴密，有條不紊；技法嫻熟，用筆細致，凝重老練，反映了晚唐時期高度的繪畫功力和杰出的藝術成就。

133. 第18窟　西壁龕内南側　天王像
莫高窟第18窟修建于晚唐，后在元代時期重修。圖中的天王像神貌精悍，戴盔披甲，怒目，威風凛凛，氣宇軒昂地立于小鬼身上。此畫設色典雅柔和，造型渾厚，神態如生，綫條清晰勁健，層次鮮明，工而不板；一切被處理得十分完美。

134. 第85窟　南壁右上角　鹿母夫人
鹿母夫人是報恩經變議論品中的一個故事情節。故事説：波羅奈國仙聖山一母鹿因食飲仙人便溺而懷孕，后産一人身鹿足之女，被仙人扶養成人，其足到之處皆生蓮花。波羅奈王出宮游獵見鹿女貌美，便迎取回宮立爲第一夫人，名爲鹿母夫人。鹿女婚后産下一朵蓮花，國王以爲不祥之物，便弃置池中。一日國王與群臣在池邊游賞，倏見池中五百蓮花瓣下各有一童男。以后五百童男長大成人，個個能力敵千人，保國土安穩。最后五百太子全部出家成爲"關支佛"。圖右側宮門外，爲國王率衆臣游於池邊，一人入池取蓮，意爲蓮花中發現五百太子。宮門内，國王與鹿女并坐於殿上，階下衆臣行禮，意爲鹿女復爲第一夫人。此畫内容豐富，故事情節曲折、生動、逼真，是敦煌石窟晚唐時期經變畫中精品。

135. 第85窟　窟頂東披　羅婆那王迎佛
羅婆那王迎佛，是楞伽經變"羅婆那王勸請品"的一個故事情節。畫面上，釋迦佛從碧綠的大海中龍宮裏出來，被楞伽城主人羅婆那王迎入城中説法；最后羅婆那王醒悟，皈依大乘佛法。此畫筆墨嚴謹，設色清麗濃重，雖咫尺小幅，但亦能表現出開闊浩渺的境界。

136. 第14窟　北壁　如意輪觀音
本窟始建于晚唐，后在宋代、清代時期重修。圖中的如意輪觀音畫像，高187厘米，寬188厘米，是密宗佛教六大觀音之一。此觀音衣著華麗，神情恬怡，儀態莊静，頭戴化佛寶冠，六臂，手托腮，持如意寶珠，持法輪，盤腿坐于寶池中的蓮花座上。此幅畫保存完整，描繪精致細微、生動活潑，是晚唐時期密宗題材的上乘之作。

137. 第85窟　窟頂　獅子蓮花藻井
獅子蓮花藻井是敦煌石窟藻井圖案的一種。此藻井繪於窟頂中央部位，屬覆鬥形狀的獅子蓮花藻井；井心内繪有卧獅、雲紋、蓮花；四周繪有回紋、菱格紋、靈鳥卷草等；藻井外繪有多彩多姿的飛天環游四周。此畫内容極爲豐富，畫面雖説繁復細密，却布置得體，層次分明；敷色沉穩雅致，是敦煌石窟藻井圖案的代表之作。

138. 第85窟　窟頂南披　帷幄夜話
這是窟頂南披《法華經變》圖中，左下角的一個帷幄夜談的故事場面。作者圍繞著二人夜談的神情進行刻劃，并精確、細致地抓住了各自聚精會神的不同情態，把一種閑適愜意的感覺被惟妙惟肖地表現出來。此畫構圖簡練，設色淡雅清秀，格調超逸。

139. 第85窟　南壁《惡友品》中　善友太子
本圖描繪的是古印度波羅奈國善友太子與利師跋國公主一段動人的愛情故事場面。故事説：波羅奈國善友太子求得一摩尼寶珠，被弟弟惡友奪取，并刺瞎了太子的雙眼。太子無奈流落爲異國（利師跋國）守園，并常在園中彈筝解悶，利師跋國公主聞筝聲而至，二人情投意合結爲夫婦。后太子雙眼復明，領公主歸國，并奪回了寶珠。圖中太子坐于綠草如茵的樹下彈筝，公主坐其對面聆聽。此圖内容豐富，故事情節曲折生動，真實地描繪了太子在異國幽居守園的生活情景。全圖畫風精巧，彩繪清潤，筆墨蒼逸勁健，屬晚唐時期遺存的精品畫之一。

140. 第14窟　北壁東側　千手鉢文殊變
圖爲莫高窟第14窟北壁東側晚唐時期繪制的一鋪千手鉢文殊變（此鋪密宗題材畫有的考述爲"千手千鉢文殊"，見《敦煌石窟内容總録P.10》，有的考述爲"千手千鉢觀音"，見《敦煌學大辭典P.62》，本書傾其前者）。此菩薩頭戴化佛冠，千手托千鉢、鉢中繪化佛，神態莊静地端坐於百寶蓮花座上。蓮座下：二龍尾纏於大海之中的須彌山腰，龍身前且有日、月高懸；蔚藍海水之中紅蓮盛開，真是情景交融，出神入化，再現了唐人爐火純青的繪畫藝術風彩。

141. 第138窟　北壁　剃度圖
剃度圖是彌勒經變情節中的一個場面。圖爲晚唐時期繪制的一幅剃度圖，它與盛唐第445窟彌勒經變中的剃度圖是一脈相承。圖中，法師正爲出家者削髮剃度，其他九人雙手合十地立於法師身后。該畫内容令人賞心悦目，繪制手法逼真細膩，敷色清新淡雅，綫條流利順暢，是晚唐時期的優秀佳作。

142. 第138窟　東壁北側　報恩經變
此窟建於光化天佑年間（公元898-907年），后經五代、元代、清代時期重修。報恩經變是敦煌石窟經變畫的一種，是依據《大方便佛報恩經》繪制而成的。它與"觀無量壽經變"和"藥師經變"同爲三聯式結構圖，尤其是發展到晚唐、五代、宋時期幾乎已成定制。此圖中央，釋迦佛結跏端坐於蓮花座上，菩薩聖衆圍繞四周，二舞伎在揮巾起舞，宮殿建築氣勢恢宏，兩旁

故事畫多姿多彩，好一派歌舞升平的佛國仙境。

143. 第156窟　北壁下部　宋國夫人出行圖
這幅宋國河内郡夫人（即張議潮夫人）出行圖，也就是宋氏夫人游春圖。繪於晚唐咸通六年間（即公元865-867年），全圖長8.3米，寬1.3米，有三部分不同的畫面相組成：即舞樂雜技爲第一部分；行李車輦、夫人騎馬游春、隨行人員的肩輿、輦、馬車，爲第二部分；衛隊相隨，榜題"宋國夫人出行圖"爲第三部分。而本圖只有第一部分，其余部分請參見文物出版社1987年出版的《中國石窟·敦煌莫高窟》第四卷P.134頁。此圖以雄偉壯闊的幅面，真實地描繪了唐時貴族游春的顯赫、富豪的氣派，同時也爲后世了解、研究唐時貴族生活提供了珍貴的歷史依據。

144. 第161窟　窟頂西披　觀音與飛天
此窟始建於晚唐，后在宋代時期重修。圖爲窟頂藻井西披的一鋪觀音圖，圖中觀音形貌端莊秀美；伎樂飛天體態優美，活潑飄逸，婀娜多姿，衣飾飄帶隨流雲飛舞。此畫内容豐富，結構完整，構圖新穎，綫條流利勁挺，是敦煌石窟唐時最優秀的一幅佳作。

145. 第196窟　西壁南側　舍利弗
本窟由何法師建于唐景福二年至乾寧元年（即公元893—894年）間，所以此窟也稱何法師窟。圖爲西壁南側勢度叉門聖變中的舍利弗；此弗神態安祥、鎮定地坐於菩提華蓋之下的高臺蓮花座上，他神色自若，變幻莫測，一會兒化作雄師吞牛，一會兒化作毗沙門天王降服夜鬼；比丘尼敲鐘報捷舍利弗獲勝，外道失敗，剃度出家，皈衣佛門。此圖保存完整，人物神態描繪生動，設色清新淡雅，是唐時壁畫的典範作品。

146. 第196窟　窟頂北披　千佛
在莫高窟壁畫中的千佛榜書題名，現多已脱落和模糊不清，而此窟千佛榜題却非常清晰可見，千佛也保存完整如新。圖中精選了窟頂北披的二十六身千佛，諸佛皆穿紅色袈裟結跏端坐於菩提華蓋下的蓮花座上；他們有的雙手捧鉢，有的作"説法相"，神色自若，各有神彩。

147. 第196窟　南壁東側下　大勢至菩薩
本圖位於第196窟南壁東側下方，名號榜題爲"南無

大勢至菩薩"。此菩薩，斜披天衣，一手托蓮花，一手握長巾，作側面像，腳踏蓮花，步履輕盈，敷色淡雅，實令人感到一種清秀的女性美。她那頭上的寶冠，透明的圓光，白晰的嫩肌，雍容的氣度，長裙和飄拂的披巾，顯現出作者超群的繪畫技巧。

148. 第196窟　中心柱佛壇背屏　花鳥紋飾

這是主尊背光上的裝飾圖案；圖案裏層層繪著石榴卷草、鳳鳥銜枝，其鳳鳥的尾巴繪的是卷草形狀，又把飛翔的鳳鳥形象融於卷草叢中，真是精妙無比。外層是由忍冬紋組成的燦爛火焰，就像是天空中五彩繽紛的彩虹，在飛卷，在流動。

五代篇（公元907─960年）

149. 第61窟　東壁門南　女供養像

該窟在元代時期重修。圖爲五代時期所繪制的一列曹氏家族的女供養人畫像；本圖只精選了在曹氏家族中具有代表性的女供養人三身：圖前一身穿回鶻服裝的爲曹議金之妻，榜題爲："故母北方大回鶻國聖天的子敕授秦國天公主隴西李氏……"；第二身穿回鶻服飾的爲曹議金之女、可漢之妻，榜題爲："姊甘州聖天可汗天公主一心供養"；第三身頭戴寶石鳳冠、穿綉花翻領長袍，戴寶石項鏈、面貼花鈿、手捧供盤供養的是曹議金另一之女，其身份也最爲顯赫，因她是于闐國王李聖天之皇后，榜題爲："姊大朝大于闐國大政大明天册全封至孝皇帝天皇后一心供養"。榜題中"故母"、"姊"稱，是因此窟爲曹議金之子曹元忠所建，故題名皆以曹元忠的口吻稱："母"、"姊"。

150. 第61窟　南壁　法華經變

法華經變，是妙法蓮華經變的略稱，屬敦煌佛教經變畫中的一種。圖爲元時所繪制的一幅法華經變畫，位於本窟南壁西起第三鋪。此畫在敦煌石窟諸多的稀世珍品中，有兩"最"之稱：一爲内容最豐富完美；二爲榜題之數最多最清晰。圖中央繪的是佛在靈鷲山説法，左右爲文殊、普賢二菩薩脅侍，菩薩聖衆、天龍八部等圍繞四周；正中上方是釋迦佛與多寶佛并坐，上方左右爲文殊、普賢二菩薩赴法會的情景，正中下方爲方便品和譬喻品。兩下角爲信解品，安樂行品。東西兩側爲化城喻品、藥草喻品和藥王菩薩本事品、妙莊嚴王本事品等。此畫保存完整，色彩豐富典雅，用筆密集細致，層次分明并富於空間深度，是熔各經變畫於一爐的佳作。

151. 第36窟　南壁西側　文殊變

此窟爲莫高窟第35窟前室，建造於五代，后經宋時重修。文殊變是敦煌佛教經變畫中的一種，也是與普賢變相對稱的題材畫。文殊菩薩的全稱爲文殊師利，傳説他是釋迦如來的九代之祖，他的弟子皆是過去諸佛，有"三世覺母"之稱，是專司智慧的菩薩。圖爲本窟僅存的文殊變中帝釋天和天龍八部等衆，其余的皆已毀壞。此畫工整嚴謹，有條不紊，保存如新，從它那濃麗艷美的色彩中仍透出唐風之遺韵。

152. 第36窟　西壁南側　龍王禮佛圖

圖爲龍王携其眷屬赴法會禮佛的情景。龍王是佛的護法神之一，他人面龍身，面相豐圓，濃眉大眼，頭戴寶冠，項飾瓔珞，長巾隨風飄舞，手托供盤於湛藍的海水之中；尤其是隨行赴會禮佛的龍女，她面相豐腴，眉清目秀，神采飄逸，猶如一美麗的少女手執香爐，風姿瀟灑地行於大海之中。藍藍的海水中紅蓮盛開，聳峙的危崖岸邊綠樹成陰，真可謂是人景交融，而又熔於一爐的神品。

153. 第61窟　西壁北側　五臺山地圖（局部）

五臺山地圖，是敦煌石窟遺存的最大一幅五臺山方圓數百裏的形象地域圖；它不但是一幅佛教史迹畫，而且還是一幅青山綠水的風景人物畫，總長13.45米，寬3.42米。全圖有僧俗人物數百之余，各種精美建築近一百八十處；各山峰和寺院皆有題名：即"中臺之頂、南臺之頂、東臺之頂、北臺之頂、西臺之頂，大建安寺、大法華寺、大佛光寺等等。圖爲寺院建築部分，其規模龐大，恢宏壯觀，并有山川秀水、僧俗來往其間。此圖場面巨大，段落分明、結構嚴密、構圖豐滿、疏密有致，不但反映了作者有高度精純的繪畫功力和超衆的藝術成就，而且還爲研究中國建築史的人們提供了重要的歷史資料。

154. 第220窟　甬道北壁　文殊變

圖爲后唐莊宗同光三年（公元925年）繪制的一鋪新樣文殊變："新"，一是以文殊菩薩爲主體，不再是以前文殊與普賢相對出現；二是原文殊變畫中的"昆侖奴"位置改繪爲于闐國王了，使現實人物直接進入了佛國世界，神人共處。圖中文殊菩薩手執如意，端坐於青獅背上的寶座上，引路童子雙手合十在前，于闐國王手握繼繩牽獅，榜題："普勸受持供養大聖感得于闐王…時"。東西兩則各繪菩薩像一身；西側榜題為："南無救苦觀世音菩薩"，東側榜題為："大聖文殊師利菩薩真容"。下部為翟奉達等翟氏家族七身男性供養人畫像。此幅畫以紅、綠、藍色彩搭配相間，色調鮮明典雅，綫描舒展勁挺，筆法嫻熟順暢，功力深厚，是五代時期的稀珍佳作，也是敦煌石窟唯一的一幅有確切紀年的珍品。

155. 第2窟（昌馬石窟） 頂部 單飛天

昌馬石窟，位於甘肅省玉門鎮九十公裏左右的昌馬河（疏勒河區域中的一段）處。昌馬石窟共有兩處；即大壩千佛洞和下窟石窟，屬敦煌石窟群之一，也是敦煌石窟藝術的重要組成部分。現存各時代洞窟十一個，但有壁畫和造像的洞窟僅存四個。窟內繪有飛天、菩薩、團花圖案等等。圖155,157,161,163為昌馬石窟第二窟主室和頂部所繪制的五代時期飛天和供養菩薩。飛天眉眼前視，身飾臂釧、手環、斜披天衣著長裙；在藍天祥雲間飛翔，其長裙、舞帶、曳帶彩雲，劃破長空。供養菩薩，神貌俊秀、莊静、有的手執鮮花，有的雙手合十在虔誠供養。該畫描繪精細，人物造型精美，衣褶轉折簡勁，設色典雅，筆墨雄渾，是昌馬石窟遺存數量不多的優秀作品。

156. 第16窟（榆林窟） 前室北側 吉祥天女

安西榆林窟第16窟修建於五代時期，在民國時期重修。圖為該窟前室北側的一幅吉祥天女畫像：吉祥天女，又稱功德天。她身著華麗，體態輕盈優美，手執香爐，回頭遥望并含有幾分少女的稚氣。此圖運用流利酣暢的綫條，淺絳的設色，簡潔的構圖，更增加了畫中秀雅清麗之氣，同時也反映了作者繪畫技能的卓而不凡。

157. 第2窟（昌馬石窟） 頂部 雙飛天

請參閱昌馬石窟第二窟頂部155圖《單飛天》文。

158. 第98窟 東壁南側 于闐國王供養像

此窟由曹議金出資修建於公元915－925年間（見敦煌學大辭典P.64），后在清代時期重修。圖為于闐（舊稱和田）國王李聖天供養像，高2.82米，高鼻大眼，蝌蚪式八字胡；頭戴漢式冕旒，身穿衮龍袍，腰圍蔽膝，雙腳由天女承托；右手執花，左手持香爐在虔誠禮佛；榜題為："大朝大寶于闐國大聖大明天子…即

是窟主"。皇后頭戴鳳冠，項飾珠寶玉串，身著大袖襦，手捧香爐供養；榜題為："大朝大于闐國大政大明天册全封至孝皇帝天皇后曹氏一心供養"。作者用輕松飄逸的綫條，濃郁典雅的設色，嚴謹的構圖，把"王者之尊"的帝王氣度刻畫的傳神如生，表現的淋灘盡致。

159. 第8窟（水峽口石窟） 供養菩薩（局部）

水峽口石窟（地方俗稱下洞子石窟）位於甘肅省安西縣城南五十公裏處的榆林河下游，現存各時期洞窟八個；即五代三個，宋代三個，西夏一個，近代一個。尚存壁畫比較好的洞窟，只有五代時期第八窟，宋代時期第三窟和第四窟。窟內繪有文殊變，西方净土變，六臂觀音，如意輪觀音，説法圖，供養菩薩，供養人畫像，千佛，飛天和各種團花圖案等。圖159,162，為水峽口石窟第八窟的兩身供養菩薩。該菩薩描繪精細，技法嫻熟，色綫遒勁，造型健美勻稱，神態脱俗如生，是水峽口石窟五代時期遺存為數不多的一幅作品。

160. 第61窟 北壁 藥師經變

圖中的藥師琉璃光佛，手持藥鉢，神態莊重而神秘地端坐在平臺中央；日光、月光菩薩脅持左右；諸天、聖衆，圍繞四周，兩根巨長的龍頭幡竿，聳立在燈塔兩側。殿前蓮花化生童子在碧綠的池水中嬉戲，舞伎在優美悦耳的樂聲中，翩翩起舞。此圖保存完整，色彩豐富雅致，構圖嚴整精妙，規模宏大，氣勢磅礴。

161. 第2窟（昌馬石窟） 主室 供養菩薩

請參閱本窟頂部155圖《單飛天》文。

162. 第八窟（水峽口石窟） 供養菩薩

請參見本窟159圖《供養菩薩局部》文。

163. 第2窟（昌馬石窟） 主室 供養菩薩

請參閱本窟頂部155圖《單飛天》文。

宋代篇（公元960－1036年）

164. 第4窟（水峽口石窟） 六臂觀音

圖為水峽口石窟第四窟殘存的一鋪六臂觀音，是密宗題材的觀音畫像之一。此觀音頭微偏，戴化佛冠，面相秀麗，神情恬静地端坐於圓光之中。服飾，手姿，

因此圖毀壞嚴重難以辯證，故不再詮釋。該畫構圖嚴謹、豐實新穎，人物形象精美，色彩雅致，運筆精工入微，是水峽口石窟極爲珍貴的一幅精品。

165. 第76窟　北壁　十一面觀音
敦煌莫高窟第76窟修建于唐代，在宋、元、清三個時期重修。十一面觀音又稱大光普照觀音，屬六觀音（即大慈、大悲、師子無畏、大光普照、天人丈夫、大梵深遠觀音）之一。此觀音十一面八臂，神態慈祥，手持蓮花、寶杖、寶杆，托日、月，施"無畏印"。位於觀音上方的三身飛天，頭戴寶冠，披巾穿裙，手捧摩尼寶珠翱翔於流雲之中；那輕盈優美的姿態，那秀麗生動的造型，清淡素雅的色彩，酣暢勁挺的綫條，用任何精美的詞句也表述不盡對她的讚美，不愧爲敦煌石窟宋時的代表。

166. 第4窟（水峽口石窟）　文殊菩薩
圖爲水峽口石窟宋時所繪的一鋪文殊變。文殊菩薩的全稱爲文殊師利，以"智慧"、"證驗"著稱。圖中的文殊菩薩：頭戴三珠寶冠，身披肩巾，項飾瓔珞，左手撫膝，右手托鉢，神態安祥地半跏坐於青獅背上的蓮座上。諸菩薩聖衆，天龍八部圍繞，幢幡隨風飄揚，浩浩蕩蕩地行於雲海之中。

167. 第17窟（榆林窟）　赴會菩薩
這個窟始建于唐代，在五代、宋代、西夏、清代時期重修；但圖中的五身赴會菩薩却是宋代所繪。此菩薩皆身著華麗，豐臉碩體，形貌端莊，有的手持鮮花，有的雙手合十，有的手握於胸前，有的手舉捻珠，真是活靈活現，千姿百態。作者以流暢遒勁的綫條塑造輕柔飄舉的衣帶，設色重彩輕施，顯得清麗華美，是吳道子畫藝的再次體現。

168. 第4窟（昌馬石窟）　供養菩薩
圖爲敦煌石窟之一的昌馬石窟第四窟的一身供養菩薩，爲宋時所繪。該菩薩右手托鉢，左手持巾端莊而立。此幅畫保存比較完整，敷色雅致，人物造型精美均稱，綫條流利遒勁，是昌馬石窟宋時的優秀作品。

169. 第76窟　東壁南側　初轉法輪
該窟初建于唐代，在宋代、元代、清代時期重修。本圖是宋時繪製的八大靈塔變之中的第三塔初轉法轉。而八大靈塔變，又是源於《佛說八大靈塔名號經》的。

塔中繪三佛雙手合十，結跏趺坐於蓮花座上。塔外左右兩側各繪三菩薩雙手合十，跪在蓮花上。榜題爲"文殊菩薩摩訶薩等來赴法會"和"普賢菩薩摩訶薩等赴法會"。此畫內容豐富，意境清新典雅，是敦煌石窟罕見的一幅珍稀佳作。

170. 第76窟　東壁北側　獼猴獻蜜
這是描繪八塔變之中第七塔獼猴獻蜜的一段故事：故事說：樹林中一有獼猴，忽見一樹無蜂而有蜜，於是便采蜜獻佛，佛受之。獼猴因佛受蜜而驚喜，不小心跌陷井中而死。此圖中部繪釋迦佛倚坐在塔內的蓮花座上，受獼猴捧鉢獻蜜；左右侍立菩薩和弟子阿難。此圖創意獨特、富有意趣，是一幅難得的佳品。

171. 第55窟　中心佛壇　彌勒三會
此窟建造于宋代，后在西夏時期重修。在敦煌石窟遺存諸多的彩塑中，爲宋時遺存甚少。圖爲莫高窟遺存比較完整的一鋪宋時期彌勒三會塑像；其善跏佛像三身，脅侍菩薩像三身，迦葉、天王、力士像各一身。這些造像，作者運用了塑、繪相結合的奇妙手法，通過衣褶、垂裾和佛坐的刻劃，使塑像顯得格外生動逼真；雖色彩已脫落變色，但仍能顯示出他們超凡脫俗的神韻。

172. 第76窟　東壁南側　釋迦降生
圖爲北宋時期所繪的八塔變中釋迦佛降生第一塔，并有榜題爲證：粤我本師釋迦牟尼佛，泯形兜率，降迹迦毗，乘白像而示應示生，躡青蓮而指天指地，净飯王捧持太子，阿私仙占相吉凶，稱雲定是法王，救度一切，果然厭四生苦，奉觀六道群迷，逾城弃生死之縈紆，雪山證菩提之滿果，此處降生第一塔也。

西夏篇（公元1036-1227年）

173. 第1窟（五個廟石窟）　南壁西側　女供養人
五個廟石窟（中國蒙古族人稱石窟爲"廟"，"五個廟"即是五個石窟，故稱之五個廟石窟），位於甘肅省肅北蒙古族自治縣城以西二十公裏處的浪彎北崖上，屬敦煌石窟群之一，是敦煌石窟藝術的重要組成部分。現存北周時期（依據敦煌研究院編《敦煌石窟內容總錄P.225、226》所劃分的年代）洞窟六個，后經五代、宋代、西夏時期重修。窟內塑有造像，繪有壁畫；其壁畫有降魔變、涅槃變、四臂觀音變、八臂觀音變、十一面千手千眼觀音變、曼陀羅、熾盛光佛、文殊變、普賢變、藥師經變、維摩詰經變、勞動叉鬥聖變、水月觀音變、供養人畫像等，內容極爲豐富。圖爲五個廟石窟第一窟南壁西側西夏時期所繪制的一身女供養人畫像：該供養人形體俊美，服飾華麗，顯然是當時上層社會的貴婦人。

174. 第409窟　東壁門南　回鶻王供養像

莫高窟第409窟始建於五代，后在回鶻、清代時期重修。圖爲回鶻國王供養像：此像面形渾圓，臉腮肥胖，高鼻梁，小眼睛；頭戴桃形雲鏤冠，身穿圓領窄袖團花龍袍，腰束革帶，腳穿氈靴，手持香爐，在虔誠禮佛。身后有八名侍從：一人執傘，兩人執扇，余者執寶劍、弓箭等。該供養像豐臉碩體的形象，是唐風形象的延續。

175. 第4窟（五個廟石窟）　東壁《净土變》中　伎樂

净土變，是諸多種類佛教畫中的一種。"净上"，在佛經中稱極樂國土，現通稱佛國世界。圖爲五個廟石窟第四窟東壁北側、西夏時期繪制的一鋪净土變中的三身伎樂。此伎樂裸上身，束短裙，手持槍，吹銅角，在狂歡起舞。其舞姿優美豪放、獨特，就是在莫高窟遺存諸多的净土變畫中也實爲少見。

176. 第3窟（五個廟石窟）　南壁西側　十一面千手千眼觀音變

此窟修建於北周時期，后在西夏時期重修。圖爲西夏時期繪制的一鋪十一面千手千眼觀音變，屬佛教密宗題材之一。該觀音頭戴化佛冠，面相豐圓秀美，神態恬靜慈祥，盤腿坐于盛開的蓮花之中。此圖已殘存不全，但仍能顯出西夏時期繪畫藝術的風彩。

177. 第409窟　東壁北側　回鶻王妃供養像

回鶻王妃供養像位於莫高窟第409窟東壁北側，身穿回鶻服裝，柳眉細目，修鼻豐頤，長髮抱面，飾耳環，兩手持花籠袖於胸前，神態莊靜地立於花氈之上虔心禮佛。

178. 第3窟（五個廟石窟）　西壁　天女

圖爲勞度叉鬥聖變畫中的四身天女。該天女面相俊秀、肌膚細膩，兩眼前視，雙手合十地行在彩雲之中。此圖保存完整，描繪人物生動，綫條細勁流暢，色彩濃淡相間，錯落有致，構圖滿而不擁塞，是西夏時期人物畫中的上品。

179. 第16窟　甬道北壁　供養菩薩

該窟修建于晚唐時期，后在西夏、清代重修。圖中所見的是第十六窟甬道北壁西夏時期繪制的四身供養菩薩：此菩薩有的手持鮮花，有的手執香爐，有的手捧花盤，腳踩蓮花而行。綠色的披巾、紅色的長裙和那精美的頭冠與瓔珞，把整幅畫面襯托的絢麗多彩。

180. 第3窟（五個廟石窟）　東壁　維摩詰像

圖中手持扇，身體前傾，雙目凝視前方，坐於帷帳之中的虬髯老人，便是維摩詰。維摩詰，是古印度毗耶離城的一位學者類的居士。他精通佛典，有很強的擅辯能力。

181. 第2窟（榆林窟）　西壁北側　水月觀音

安西榆林窟第二窟開鑿於西夏時期，后在元代、清代重修。水月觀音，因對月臨水，倚石沐風，有高人雅士風度，所以深得中國文人士大夫之類的人喜愛。圖181、183二鋪西夏繪制的水月觀音，寶冠峨髻，衣袍寬松，悠閑地倚坐在青石之上，姿態瀟灑。上有彩雲追月，下有綠水漾波，月影岩石嶙峋，净瓶纖枝弱柳，綠葉飛絮，身后修竹蔥翠，腳旁荷花芬香；清風徐來，披巾微蕩，一邊兒的童子乘祥雲飄然而來，真是奇景妙境。正如唐人白居易《畫水月菩薩贊》詩中所寫的那樣："静綠波上，虛白光中，一睹其像，萬緣皆空"。

182. 第7窟（東千佛洞）　東壁上方　飛天

東千佛洞，位於甘肅省安西縣橋了鄉南三十五公裏處的峽谷兩岸上，屬敦煌石窟群之一，是敦煌石窟藝術的重要組成部分。現存各時期有壁畫、塑像的洞窟八個；即東岩三個、西岩五個。窟內塑有部分造像，繪有壁畫，其壁畫有經變畫、尊像畫、密宗畫像、供養人畫像和裝飾圖案等。圖爲東千佛洞第七窟東壁上方西夏時期繪制的一身飛天，該飛天上身半裸，斜披綢帶，露左肩，下穿長褲短裙，赤足，身飾瓔珞、臂釧。回首前視，右手上舉，左手散花。真是盡善盡美，神韵怡人。

183. 第2窟（榆林窟）　西壁南側　水月觀音

請參見181圖本窟西壁北側《水月觀音》文。

184. 第2窟（東千佛洞）　唐僧取經

這是描繪唐玄奘和"猴行者"（玄奘"行狀"中的石

槃陀）師徒二人，遠隔水岸，參拜觀音的情景，也是后來《西游記》書中所述"唐玄奘"去西天取經的故事。不過此時《西游記》還尚未問世，因此圖比《西游記》書中所描述的要早幾百年，也是敦煌石窟遺存最古老的一幅唐僧取經圖之一。

185. 第2窟（東千佛洞） 南壁 菩提樹觀音
該菩薩一手向上舉起，一手下垂倒握净瓶，施甘露於餓鬼，身軀彎曲，形成了優美的舞姿狀。遠處藍天白雲，近處緑水蕩漾，菩提樹鮮花盛開，真不愧爲仙人居住的地方。此圖意境幽雅寧静，人物造型奇特，體態秀美，墨色秀潤明麗，運筆精工入微，是敦煌石窟西夏時期罕見的一幅菩薩珍品。

186. 第1窟（五個廟石窟） 菩薩
該菩薩面相清秀，兩眼前視，頭束髻，戴寶冠，長發披肩，雙臂生翼，手持扇，著天衣，其綠色巾帶貼肩而下垂，結跏端坐於蓮花座上。神態慈祥、閑適悠然。

187. 第2窟（東千佛洞） 北壁 水月觀音
水月觀音，是民間的通俗之稱，她的本稱應爲落迦山觀音。落迦山，是著名的佛教名山聖地。據佛籍史料記載，此山即是觀音菩薩所居住的地方。圖爲東千佛洞第二窟北壁西夏時期繪制的一鋪水月觀音圖；此觀音高雅素潔，相貌秀美，寶冠峨髻，衣袍寬松、安閑地倚坐在岩石上凝思。岩石上的净瓶，插著柳枝，山后翠竹青青，河水中蓮荷芬芳，小河對岸唐玄奘雙手合十禮拜，猴行者一手牽馬、一手舉起眺望。此畫描繪工整，設色豐富典雅，不愧爲西夏時期觀音畫中的優秀之作。

188. 第3窟（榆林窟） 西壁南側 唐僧取經
請參見184圖東千佛洞第二窟《唐僧取經》文。

189. 第3窟（榆林窟） 西壁南側 普賢變
圖中層層山巒竟相叠嶂，叢林秀木參差其間，樓閣依山傍水，山徑盤曲環繞，普賢菩薩乘象半跏坐於蓮花座上，與菩薩聖衆游於茫茫的雲海之中。畫中有可行的山間小道，有可看的仙人浮游雲間，有可游的山川秀水，又有可居的蕭寺樓閣，真是一幅奇圖妙景。此畫用酣暢淋灕的水墨綫繪制烟雲，以大斧劈皴繪山岩、危崖峭壁，再薄施淡彩讓水色流雲、人物貫通一體，使整幅畫面具有朦朧的神秘之感；這皆是作者取多家

之長的技藝用於佛畫創作的結晶。

190. 第3窟（榆林窟） 西壁北側 文殊變
此鋪文殊變畫的不同之處，就是它那氣勢恢宏的五臺山山水背景。背景中山嶺縱橫、彩虹斜挂、樓閣巍峨、烟波浩淼，雲氣飄渺；文殊菩薩便安坐在獅子蓮座上，與諸菩薩聖衆行於這一派仙山雲海的壯麗奇景之中。此圖以繁瑣飽滿的構圖，將山石樹木、亭臺樓閣、人物幾乎填滿全局，只留下較小的空間。但畫滿而不悶，繁而不亂。經過作者精心的布置，將雲烟、小溪及山下的空白，作巧妙的縈回、牽引、避讓，使這渾拙雄厚的巨壑重巒之間透出空靈之氣。圖中的勾、皴、點、染、擦，運用的非常靈活精妙。筆調凝重老練，再加上層層積墨積色，更使得畫意奧境奇闊，緬邈幽深。

191. 第2窟（東千佛洞） 南壁 水月觀音
請參閱東千佛洞第二窟北壁187圖《水月觀音》文。

192. 第2窟（東千佛洞） 東壁北側 供養菩薩
圖爲東千佛洞第二窟東壁北側西夏時期繪制的三面八臂觀音變中一身供養菩薩：該菩薩相貌秀美端莊，雙手合十，盤腿坐在蓮座上虔心供養。

193. 第2窟（東千佛洞） 北甬道 藥師佛
藥師佛，也稱藥師琉璃光如來，有醫王佛之稱。圖中的藥師佛左手托玻璃藥鉢，右手執杖立於蓮花座上，二僧人雙手合十侍立左右。此畫構圖簡潔准確，畫風精巧，彩繪清潤，筆墨蒼逸勁健，是西夏時期的上乘之作。

194. 第5窟（東千佛洞） 緑度母
緑度母，是二十一尊聖救度母（即多羅觀音）的化身像之一。圖中的緑度母周身綠色，頭戴寶冠，項飾瓔珞，一手持花，一手置膝，左腿曲，右腿下垂，坐于蓮花金剛座上。

195. 第328窟 東壁北側 供養菩薩
圖中的兩身供養菩薩和真人大小相近，他們面相方圓，體型壯碩，清晰的土紅綫勾勒出臉形、五官和手足，人體基本不暈染，有較強的平面裝飾效果。綠色的披巾、紅色的長裙和那精美的頭冠、瓔珞，使整個畫面清新明快，絢麗多彩。

196. 第7窟（東千佛洞） 接引佛

接引佛，即是阿彌陀佛的立像，意爲信徒們念佛行善臨終時由阿彌陀佛、觀世音菩薩、大勢至菩薩等聖眾，前去接引他們入極樂世界，故稱接引佛。圖爲東千佛洞西夏時期所繪制的一幅引接佛；此佛身披袈裟、跣足立於蓮座上，眾弟子、菩薩、侍立前后左右，神將護衛，二菩薩抬著一朵盛開的大蓮花在天宮中俯視人間。此圖創意新穎，描繪工細，色彩淡雅，是敦煌石窟東千佛洞遺存較完整的一幅珍品。

197. 第 306 窟　南壁西側　脅侍菩薩
此窟修建于隋代，在五代和西夏時期重修。圖爲本窟南壁説法圖中西側西夏所繪的一身脅侍菩薩。該菩薩兩眼微睜，寧静閑適，左腿向下舒展，雙手抱右膝，半跏坐于香案后的蓮座上。此畫取法五代、宋人之傳承，于遒勁之中透出秀雅之氣。

198. 第 1 窟（五個廟石窟）　南壁　男供養人畫像
供養人，就是籌款出資建窟或維修洞窟的人（即建窟修窟的窟主），并在自己出資建的窟中繪上自己的像。圖爲五個廟石窟第一窟南壁西夏時期所繪的一身男供養人畫像；該供養人頭戴雲縷冠，身穿圓領窄袖袍，腰束帶，脚蹬靴，雙手合十，虔誠供養。

199. 第 2 窟（東千佛洞）　東壁北側　三面八臂觀音
圖爲敦煌石窟群之一的東千佛洞第二窟東壁北側西夏時期繪制的一身三面八臂觀音像，屬藏傳佛教密宗題材。此圖内函豐富，繪制精細，色彩艷麗而不俗，是一幅珍貴的西夏時期密宗繪畫作品。

200. 第 2 窟（東千佛洞）　北壁　菩提樹觀音
請參閱東千佛洞第二窟南壁185圖《菩提樹觀音》文。

元代篇（公元 1227 — 1368 年）

201. 第 4 窟（榆林窟）　南壁東側　白度母
這個窟開鑿于元代，后在清代重修。圖爲元時所繪的一鋪度母菩薩，屬藏傳佛教。度母菩薩有青、紅、綠、白等色之分，可顯現二十一相，但一般常見到的是綠度母和白度母菩薩，本圖即爲白度母菩薩。該菩薩身穿黑短裙、飾項圈、瓔珞、臂釧，兩眼前視，端莊地坐于蓮花寶座上；寶座下有五尊手勢各異的菩薩端坐在五朵蓮花之中。此圖保存完整，造型、構圖、暈染、敷色、布局都十分獨特，是研究藏傳佛教的珍貴形象資料。

202. 第 3 窟　北壁　千手千眼觀音
圖爲本窟北壁的一鋪千手千眼觀音變，是六觀音之一。千手千眼意爲觀音觀照，護持和救度眾生，法力廣大。此觀音面相俊秀，十一面，頭戴化佛冠，千手繪千眼，神態莊静地跣足立於蓮座上。兩側以對稱的方式繪著辯才天、婆藪仙、吉祥天女、火頭金剛等形像；上方繪二飛天持花供養。作者綜合了北魏、隋唐的繪畫技巧，把觀音的慈善，金剛的威猛，吉祥天女的端莊，婆藪仙的深沉，飛天的美姿皆表現得淋灕盡致。

203. 第 61 窟　甬道南壁　熾盛光佛
圖爲該窟甬道南壁元代所繪制的一幅"熾盛光佛"；是依據《佛説無比大威德金輪佛頂熾盛光消災吉祥陀羅尼經》繪制而成的。佛經説：佛身毛孔能放出熾盛的光明，故稱之爲"熾盛光佛"。此佛手執金輪，端莊地坐在大輪車的蓮座上，五星十二宮和二十八宿等諸神隨游雲海之中。這幅畫内容豐富多彩，構圖有致，布局取舍得體，用筆頗見功力，是元時最優秀的珍品之一。

204. 第 3 窟　南壁　千手千眼觀音
請參見圖 202，本窟北壁《千手千眼觀音》文。

205. 第 465 窟　北壁中部　眷屬
該眷屬裸體，高髻，三目，飾瓔珞、環釧。左手持法器，右手持物，右脚曲於身前，左脚踏在蓮花座上的人形上。此圖造型獨特，畫風細密精致，色彩雖已脱落，但仍能顯現它當年的藝術風彩。

206. 第 465 窟　窟頂南披　供養菩薩
該菩薩上身裸露，有項圈、臂釧、手鐲和佩飾，下著短裙，手持蓮花，雙膝相叠而坐；整個人體顯出矯健、靈活、充滿生氣。此畫用鐵綫描勾勒，人體顯得細膩而更富有彈性。淺藍色的人體在豐富多彩的背光和頭光襯托下，格外醒目。深赭色的瓔珞和石綠色的飄帶爲此畫增添了華美的色感。

207. 第 465 窟　東壁門南　護法
圖爲莫高窟第465窟東壁門南《護法曼陀羅》中的護法神；此護法神，紅發、三目、裸上身，兩臂屈於胸前，手持法器，兩腿叉開作蹲姿狀。此畫人物造型奇特，神態刻劃如生，用筆細密而蒼健，是元時畫中之精品。

208. **第465窟　南壁中部　雙身曼陀羅**
曼陀羅，梵文音譯。它有兩種含意，即一爲壇，二爲道場。據《探玄記》二十曰：“曼陀羅，雲，道場也，圓、壇也”；又《演密鈔》二曰”曼陀羅，聖賢集會之處，萬德交歸之所”。此圖中部繪雙身主尊，男尊身青色，裸上身，束短裙，三頭六臂，三目；手持鉢，持金剛、持劍、持輪、持蓮花，於女尊相抱。女尊，身藍身，裸體，三目，頭高髻；手持輪、持蓮花、持金剛，持劍，於男尊相抱。此畫人物神態描繪精妙，創意獨特，寓意含蓄。

209. **第95窟　南壁西側　長眉羅漢**
長眉羅漢是十六羅漢之首的長者，名爲賓頭盧；是依據唐玄奘法師所譯的《犬阿羅漢難提密多羅所説法住記》繪制而成的。羅漢的像貌各不相同，圖中的羅漢面相慈祥，長眉過膝，朵頤隆鼻，身披袈裟，雙手扶杖，身前一弟子雙手捧侍長眉，坐於竹靠背似的椅子上。此畫形象傳神、古僕、氣氛和諧，展現了師徒之間和藹可親的真摯感情。

210. **第465窟　南壁東側　大幻金剛**
大幻金剛是釋迦佛爲調伏欲界衆生顯現的雙身像之一。通身藍色，三面十六臂。圖爲南壁東側的雙身像，兩主尊全裸，其男尊通身藍色，左手持弓右手搭箭與佛母相抱；佛母全身紅棕色，左右手持弓搭箭與金剛相抱。此圖章法嚴密，構圖嚴謹，形態描繪逼真，筆墨蒼郁灑脱，實爲高手之筆。

211. **第6窟（東千佛洞）　北壁　文殊變**
文殊，全稱爲文殊師利。他的畫像是諸多的菩薩畫像之一，常見形式一般和普賢相對出現，而本圖卻例外；作者沒有采用文殊與普賢相對出現的慣用手法，僅以文殊像爲主體，山巒迭嶂、遠嶺烟樹爲襯托。此菩薩面相方圓，頭飾三珠寶冠，披肩巾，手執如意，神態莊重，結跏趺坐在青獅背上的蓮座上。

212. **第465窟　北壁　觀喜金剛**
該窟壁畫内容在敦煌石窟中實屬罕見，是依據藏傳佛教密宗題材繪制而成的。在藏傳佛教中，佛屬于自性爲法身，稱之自性輪身。菩薩顯現真實身，是以法度人，稱之正法輪身。明王是授佛的教令，顯現忿怒形，摧伏一切怨敵淫魔，稱之教令輪身。圖爲北壁中部的雙身佛合抱像，也稱之歡喜金剛。金剛通身藍色，高

大雄壯，項戴骷髏珠串，左右側各有三頭三目，十六臂，皆持鉢，與佛母相抱。佛母身爲赭紅色，一面兩臂，三目，裸身，右手持月形勾刀與金剛相抱。此畫運筆犀利，酣暢淋灘，綫條恣肆，含蓄蘊藉。具有薩迦派的獨特藝術風格，是一幅不可多得的藏傳佛教密宗題材珍品。

213. **第2窟（東千佛洞）　東壁南側　供養菩薩**
圖爲西夏時期（據敦煌研究院編《敦煌石窟内容總録》斷代）繪制的一身供養菩薩；該菩薩的相貌，坐姿均于莫高窟第465窟南披元代所繪的一身供養菩薩相似。此圖保存完整，描繪精細，設色濃艷，形象矯柔秀美而充滿靈氣，是敦煌石窟遺存不多的密教題材畫之一。

絹畫篇

214. **女供養人**
圖爲《樹下説法圖》中佛陀右下角的一身女供養像：該供養像容顏豐腴，椎髻，穿長裙，手捧蓮花，雙膝長跪，虔心供養。

215. **樹下説法圖**
這幅畫繪于初唐，屬絹本畫。高139厘米，寬101.7厘米，是莫高窟藏經洞（今第十七窟）遺存的絹本畫中年代最久的作品之一。圖爲樹下説法圖：佛居中結跏端坐在蓮座上説法，兩側有比丘、衆菩薩聽法。下方左右各繪一供養菩薩，該菩薩有的雙手捧蓮花，有的雙手捧香爐在虔誠供養。此畫結構嚴謹，描繪細致、綫條流暢，色彩豐富、艷麗，亦屬唐時絹本畫中的精品之作。

216. **舍利弗**
這幅絹本畫極爲珍貴，在敦煌石窟遺存的絹畫中僅此一幅。該畫繪于唐代（八一九世紀），高95.9厘米，寬51.8厘米。圖爲《靈鷲山釋迦説法圖》中的舍利弗。此弗身著青色袈裟，一手籠袖，一手持香爐恭敬地立於佛旁。

217. **報恩經變**
此畫繪于唐代（九世紀前半），高160.8厘米，寬121.6厘米，是莫高窟藏經洞内遺存的絹本畫中保存較完整、内容極爲豐富的一幅珍品。圖中繪的是《大方便佛報恩經變》的變相；左側是孝養品，描述須闍提太子割肉孝養雙親的故事，左側上端是鹿母本生的故

事，下方是善友和惡友太子的故事；圖中央是充滿光明喜樂的釋迦净土；上方是雄偉壯觀的佛寺大殿。該畫描繪精細，整齊大方，色彩濃施艷抹，雖因年久脱落變色，但仍有富麗堂皇的光彩。

218. 水星
圖中頭戴猴形冠，身著女裝，一手執筆，一手拿紙薄的是《熾盛光佛》圖中的五星神之一水星（即辰星）。

219. 熾盛光佛
此圖繪于唐代乾寧四年（公元897年）。高80.4厘米，寬55.4厘米，是依據《佛説無比大威德金輪佛頂熾盛光佛消灾吉祥陀羅尼經》繪制而成的；于莫高窟元代61窟甬道南壁所繪的壁畫内容基本相同。圖中的"熾盛光佛"身穿紅色袈裟，佛光四射，端莊地坐於雙輪牛車上的蓮花寶座中，車尾旌旗飄揚，五星神二面簇擁行於雲海之中，其氣氛既莊重，而又神秘。

220. 金星
圖中頭戴鳥冠，身穿白色女裝，手抱琵琶者是《熾盛光佛》圖中的五星神之一金星（即太白金星）。

221. 土星
圖中頭束發，戴牛冠，上身裸露，跣足，手執錫杖繮繩者是《熾盛光佛》圖中的五星神之一土星（即鎮星）。

222. 九龍灌頂
圖爲九龍吐清净的温凉二水給太子沐浴的情景。胖乎乎的悉達太子站在俯蓮座的仰蓮盆内，五宫女正忙於侍奉著。此圖結構簡潔，筆法拙厚、渾雄而凝重。

223. 離别
這是描繪悉達多太子出家修道，一日夜半，乘白馬和車匿出城至深山并與車匿，白馬告别的感人場面。圖中太子坐於岩石上，車匿掩面而泣，白馬跪拜向太子辭行。此景傷感動人，但也反映了太子與車匿、白馬之間的熾熱融洽之情。

224. 鹿女
這是一幅描繪《議論品》中鹿女足下生蓮的故事圖畫。故事説：當時南窟和北窟都住有仙人。南窟仙人便溺于泉邊，被母鹿食之而懷孕生鹿女。鹿女長大成人，一日不慎熄滅了火種，鹿女便到北窟仙人處借

之，她足到之處生朵朵蓮花。圖中即是鹿女足下步步生蓮的情景。

225. 童子
圖爲三個天真無邪的童子，在盛開的蓮花中嬉戲。畫中構圖簡括，綫描粗壯有力，設色濃郁艷麗，是唐風時尚的表現。

226. 藥師佛
這幅精美的絹畫，繪于唐代（9世紀后半），高84厘米，寬49.1厘米，今存法國吉美博物館。圖中藥師如來佛身穿衲衣，披田相紅色袈裟，左手托鉢，右手持錫杖，神情莊静地立於白色的蓮花座上。兩僧人一個雙手合十，一個手拿經卷神情恭敬地侍立佛的左右兩側。圖的右上方畫題爲："奉爲亡過小娘子李氏畫藥師佛壹軀永充供養兼慶贊記"。作品用挺拔的鐵描綫勾勒衣紋，施色濃艷華麗，反映了唐人的審美情趣。

227. 千手千眼觀音
圖爲北宋太平興國六年（公元981年）繪制的一幅千手千眼觀音絹畫，縱189.4厘米，橫124厘米；今存法國吉美博物館。此觀音頭戴化佛冠，面相豐腴，端莊地跣足立於蓮花座上。華嚴、不空羂索、如意輪等菩薩聖衆圍繞四周。下方左側繪樊繼壽及侍從的供養像，右側是地藏菩薩和道明和尚，中間爲二十四行文字的"功德記"。此畫保存完整，内容豐富，敷色艷麗，綫條細膩酣暢，亦爲絹畫之中精品。

228. 天王行道圖
此絹畫繪于唐代（9世紀），高37.6厘米，寬26.6厘米，今存英國博物館。圖中的天王頭戴寶冠，濃眉大眼、八字胡，雙肩火焰飄浮，一手持戟，一手托塔，鎧甲戎裝，威風凛凛地携衆神行在雲海之中。

229. 降魔成道圖
這是敦煌莫高窟藏經洞（今17窟）遺存的絹本畫，繪於五代（10世紀前半）。現存法國吉美博物館，縱144.4厘米，橫113厘米。圖中釋迦佛面相豐腴，右袒金色袈裟，手結降魔印，神態莊嚴地端坐於華蓋下的蓮座上，魔軍惡鬼姿態各异地圍繞四周。此畫人物繁多但錯落有致，構圖嚴謹，描繪細致，色彩豐富亮麗，是五代時期絹畫之上品。